COUNS TEACHER, AND GUIDE

A STUDY ON THE HOLY SPIRIT

by William Farrand

AN INDEPENDENT-STUDY TEXTBOOK

Developed in Cooperation with the ICI University Staff

Instructional Development Specialist: Juanita Cunningham Blackburn

Illustrator: Rick Allen

ICI University Press
6300 North Belt Line Road
Irving, Texas 75063
USA

Address of the local ICI office in your area:

First Edition 1983
Third Edition 1996 9/96 3M LR

S3331E-91

ISBN 1-56390-032-7

TABLE OF CONTENTS

THE ICI CHRISTIAN SERVICE PROGRAM

This is one of 18 courses (subjects) that make up the ICI Christian Service Program. The symbol at the left is a guide for order of study in the series, which is divided into three units of six courses each. *Counselor, Teacher, and Guide* is Course 3 in Unit III. You will benefit by studying the courses in their proper order.

Study materials in the Christian Service Program have been prepared in a self-teaching format especially for Christian workers. These courses provide a student with Bible knowledge and skills needed for practical Christian service. You may study this course in order to receive credit toward a certificate or for personal enrichment.

ATTENTION

Please read the course introduction very carefully. It is important that you follow these instructions so you can achieve the goals of the course, and be prepared for the student reports.

Address all correspondence concerning the course to your ICI instructor at the address printed on the copyright page of this study guide.

COURSE INTRODUCTION

Your Friend, the Holy Spirit

Near the end of Jesus' ministry on earth He told His disciples that the time was coming when He would no longer be with them. Then He said:

> And I will ask the Father, and he will give you another Counselor to be with you forever—the Spirit of truth. The world cannot accept him, because it neither sees him nor knows him. But you know him, for he lives with you and will be in you (John 14:16-17).

Jesus was talking about the Holy Spirit, the Third Person in the Trinity. God the Father sent His Son, Jesus, into the world to show us what God is like. When Jesus ascended back to His Father in heaven, He sent the Holy Spirit to abide in the hearts of believers. The Holy Spirit reveals Christ to us. Although we cannot see the Holy Spirit, we can sense His presence and direction in our lives as we yield ourselves to His control.

There are a number of symbols for the Holy Spirit in the Bible: *wind* (Acts 2:2); a gentle *dove* (Matthew 3:16-17); *fire* (Matthew 3:11); and *water* (John 7:37-39). These symbols represent different aspects of the Holy Spirit in His ministry to us. He is a dove, a gentle helping Friend who walks alongside us. He is living water springing up from within us. He is a holy fire that relines our spiritual life, convicting us of all that is inconsistent with our new life in Christ. He is a powerful wind, moving in miraculous, supernatural manifestations through Spirit-filled believers.

In these lessons we will introduce you to your Friend, the Holy Spirit. He is a personal Friend, with the ability to reason, to feel, and to make decisions. He is a divine Friend, having all the attributes of God. He is a helping Friend who will stand beside you in every circumstance.

The Holy Spirit is a powerful Friend, who is active in Creation, in communicating God's message to man, and in regenerating lost and dying souls. He is also a practical Friend, who helps us in our worship, in our ministry to one another, and by forming the image of Christ in us.

We pray that these lessons will motivate you to become personally involved with your divine Friend, the Holy Spirit, so that you may grow in spiritual maturity from day to day, and so that you may experience the unlimited rewards of the Spirit-filled life!

Course Description

Counselor, Teacher, and Guide: A Study on the Holy Spirit is an introductory course on attributes of the Holy Spirit and His activities in the world from Creation to the present. He is presented as a personal, powerful, and practical Friend who abides in the Spirit-filled believer and through him reveals Jesus Christ to the world. With the pentecostal experience of baptism in the Holy Spirit, the believer is empowered for witness, service, and holy living. The course is a practical guide to the student who desires a Spirit-filled life.

Course Objectives

When you finish this course you should be able to:

1. List the divine and personal attributes of the Holy Spirit.
2. Describe the Holy Spirit's involvement in Creation, in communication with man, and in regeneration.
3. Understand the meaning of spiritual worship, the baptism in the Holy Spirit, the gifts of the Spirit, and the fruit of the Spirit.

4. Recognize the value of a Spirit-filled life and desire that the Holy Spirit will manifest Jesus Christ in your life.

Textbooks

You will use *Counselor, Teacher, and Guide* by William Farrand as both the textbook and study guide for this course. The Bible is the only other textbook required Scriptures quoted are from the *New International Version*, 1978 edition, unless otherwise noted.

Study Time

How much time you actually need to study each lesson depends in part on your knowledge of the subject and the strength of your study skills before you begin the course. The time you spend also depends on the extent to which you follow directions and develop skills necessary for independent study. Plan your study schedule so that you spend enough time to reach the objectives stated by the author of the course and your personal objectives as well.

Lesson Organization and Study Pattern

Each lesson includes: 1) lesson title, 2) opening statement, 3) lesson outline, 4) lesson objectives, 5) learning activities, 6) key words, 7) lesson development including study questions, 8) self-test (at the end of the lesson development), and 9) answers to the study questions.

The lesson outline and objectives will give you an overview of the subject, help you to focus your attention on the most important points as you study, and tell you what you should learn.

Most of the study questions in the lesson development can be answered in spaces provided in this study guide. Longer answers should be written in a notebook. As you write the answers in your notebook, be sure to record the number and title of the lesson. This will help you in your review for the unit student report.

Do not look ahead at the answers until you have given your answer. If you give your own answers, you will remember what you study much better. After you have answered the study questions, check your answers with those given at the end of the lesson. Then correct those you did not answer correctly. The answers are not given in the usual numerical order so that you will not accidentally see the answer to the next question.

These study questions are very important. They will help you to remember the main ideas presented in the lesson and to apply the principles you have learned.

How to Answer Questions

There are different kinds of study questions and self-test questions in this study guide. Below are samples of several types and how to answer them. Specific instructions will be given for other types of questions that may occur.

A *MULTIPLE-CHOICE* question or item asks you to choose an answer from the ones that are given.

Example

1 A week has a total of
a) 10 days.
b) 7 days.
c) 5 days.

The correct answer is *b) 7 days.* In your study guide, make a circle around *b)* as shown here:

1 A week has a total of
a) 10 days.
(b) 7 days.
c) 5 days.

(For some multiple-choice items, more than one answer will be correct. In that case, you would circle the letter in front of each correct answer.)

A *TRUE-FALSE* question or item asks you to choose which of several statements are TRUE.

2 Which statements below are TRUE?

a The Bible has a total of 120 books.

(b) The Bible is a message for believers today.

c All of the Bible authors wrote in the Hebrew language.

(d) Holy Spirit inspired the writers of the Bible.

Statements **b** and **d** are true. You would make a circle around these two letters to show your choices, as you see above.

A *MATCHING* question or item asks you to match things that go together, such as names with descriptions, or Bible books with their authors.

Example

3 Write the number for the leader's name in front of each phrase that describes something he did.

..1.. **a** Received the Law at Mt. Sinai	1) Moses
..2.. **b** Led the Israelites across Jordan	2) Joshua
..2.. **c** Marched around Jericho	
..1.. **d** Lived in Pharaoh's court	

Phrases **a** and **d** refer to Moses, and phrases **b** and **c** refer to Joshua. You would write **1** beside **a** and **d**, and **2** beside **b** and **c**, as you see above.

Ways to Study This Course

If you study this ICI course by yourself, all of your work can be completed by mail. Although ICI has designed this course for you to study on your own, you may also study it in a group or class. If you do this, the instructor may give you added instructions besides those in the course. If so, be sure to follow his instructions.

Possibly you are interested in using the course in a home Bible study group, in a class at church, or in a Bible school. You will find both the subject content and study methods excellent for these purposes.

Unit Student Reports

In the back of your study guide are located the unit student reports and answer sheets. These are to be completed according to the instructions included in the course and in the instructions in the unit student reports. After you have completed the answer sheets, send them to your instructor for grading and suggestions regarding your work.

Certificate

Upon the successful completion of the course and the final grading of the unit answer sheets by your ICI instructor, you will receive your Certificate of Award. Or, if you prefer, you may study this course for personal enrichment without receiving a certificate.

Author of This Course

William F. Farrand writes from much experience as a pastor, evangelist, Bible school instructor, and administrator. He was ordained as a minister of the gospel in 1951. For 26 years he has served as a missionary in Ceylon and the Philippines. He was a professor at Ceylon Bible Institute for three years, at Bethel Bible Institute in Manila for ten years. Currently he is at Immanuel Bible College in Cebu, Republic of Philippines. He has held the positions of business manager, academic dean, and president in these schools.

Mr. Farrand earned a Bible diploma at Eastern Bible Institute in Pennsylvania, and his M.A. in Bible and theology at the Assemblies of God Graduate School in Springfield, Missouri. He has also studied at the University of Philippines, Central

Bible College, Asian Theological Seminary, and Fuller Theological Seminary.

Your ICI Instructor

Your ICI instructor will be happy to help you in any way possible if you have any questions about the course or the unit student reports, please feel free to ask him. If several people want to study this course together, ask about special arrangements for group study.

God bless you as you begin to study *Counselor, Teacher, and Guide.* May it enrich your life and Christian service and help you fulfill more effectively your part in the body of Christ.

Additional Helps

Other materials are available for use with this Individual Study Textbook, including supplemental audio cassettes, video cassettes, an Instructor's Guide, and an Instructor's Packet (for instructor's use only). Consult the Evangelism, Discipleship, and Training Manual.

UNIT ONE

THE HOLY SPIRIT: A PERSONAL FRIEND

RALLEN

LESSON 1

A COMPLETE PERSON

When my family and I first arrived in the Philippines, where I was to assume the direction of Immanuel Bible College, the staff and student body held a reception for us. All kinds of local delicacies were served and the entertainment was very enjoyable. I heard one of the students say, "I really like receptions." It was a day to be remembered.

I wonder how I would have felt if they had forgotten the purpose of the reception. But they didn't. Someone stood and said, "We have enjoyed the food and entertainment, but this is not the main reason we are here. We have come to welcome our new president, who will be with us for the next school term."

Later as I thought about it I was reminded of testimonies of another much more important reception—receiving the baptism of the Holy Spirit. Many people talk about the *blessing* they received when they were baptized in the Holy Spirit, but they fail to mention the divine *Person* involved.

The Holy Spirit is a *complete Person.* Because He is a complete Person, we can have a person-to-Person relationship with Him that is totally satisfying, one that will meet our deepest needs and prepare us for our place in the kingdom of God. In this lesson we will explore scriptural evidences of the *personality* of the Holy Spirit and their implications for us.

lesson outline

His Personal Qualities
His Personal Offices
His Personal Designations
Our Personal Relationship

lesson objectives

When you finish this lesson you should be able to:

- Support the statement: "The Holy Spirit is a complete Person" by discussing His personal designations, His personal qualities, and His personal offices.
- Describe the kind of person-to-Person relationship we can have with the Holy Spirit because He is a Person.

learning activities

1. Read the course introduction at the beginning of this study guide. This will help you to understand the purpose of the course and how to respond to the study exercises in each lesson.

2. Study the lesson outline and lesson objectives for lesson 1. These will help you identify the things you should try to learn as you study the lesson.
3. Read the lesson and do the exercises in the lesson development. Write answers to questions in this study guide where space is provided. Where longer answers are required, use a notebook. Check your answers with those given at the end of the lesson.
4. Your understanding of the key words is essential to a good understanding of the lesson content. Check the glossary at the back of this study guide for definitions of any key words you do not know.
5. Take the self-test at the end of the lesson and check your answers carefully. Review any items you answer incorrectly. The answers are given at the back of the study guide.

key words

administrative	elders	manifested
blasphemy	emotional	marred
commissioning	grieve	misconduct
contend	illuminates	neuter
counselor	intercedes	oriented
designation	intimate	sensitive

lesson development

HIS PERSONAL QUALITIES

Objective 1. *Select true statements which describe evidences of the personality of the Holy Spirit.*

Introduction

When you think of a *person* you probably think of a human being much like yourself who has the ability to think and feel and make decisions. The ability to know, feel, and choose was given to us by God, and we are made in His image. He is the *ideal* of what a complete and perfect person is, and we are simply the marred copies. So it is not our purpose to say that the Holy Spirit is a Person because He is like *us*. Rather, our personality is patterned after the divine model; therefore, we have the same essential qualities of Personality: the ability to think, feel, and decide.

All of the qualities which indicate personality are found in the Holy Spirit. He is a living being. In fact, as we shall see, He is the source and giver of life, and one of His names is "the Spirit of Life" (Romans 8:2).

Because we usually think of a person as someone with a visible physical body, we miss the real meaning of the word *person*, which refers to the foregoing qualities of personality: the ability to know, to feel, and to choose. Does the personality of the Holy Spirit mean more to you in your daily life than if He were merely an impersonal force? Because He is a complete Person who can think, feel, and choose, He is the perfect channel for communicating your desires to God and God's will to you!

1 Based upon the discussion in this section, which of the following completions is best? When I say that the Holy Spirit is a Person, I mean that
a) He is like me.
b) He has the essential qualities of personality.
c) He is a physical as well as a spiritual being.
d) He is a spiritual being.

Let's examine each of the qualities of personality of the Holy Spirit, and think about their significance for us.

The Ability to Know

Objective 2. *Analyze given Scriptures to determine what they reveal about the Holy Spirit's ability to know.*

One of the primary qualities of personality is the ability to *know*. We associate this ability with the mind. God's Word states that the Holy Spirit acts with intelligence and wisdom:

> And he who *searches* our hearts knows the *mind* of the Spirit, because the Spirit intercedes for the saints in accordance with God's will (Romans 8:27).
>
> The Spirit *searches* all things, even the deep things of God. For who among men knows the thoughts of a man except the man's spirit within him? In the same way no one knows the thoughts of God except the Spirit of God (1 Corinthians 2:10-11).

In this second Scripture, the apostle Paul compares a man's ability to know man with the same personal quality in the Holy Spirit in the spiritual realm. Note that this personal quality is related to the man's spirit, which will endure, and not to his body, which will die.

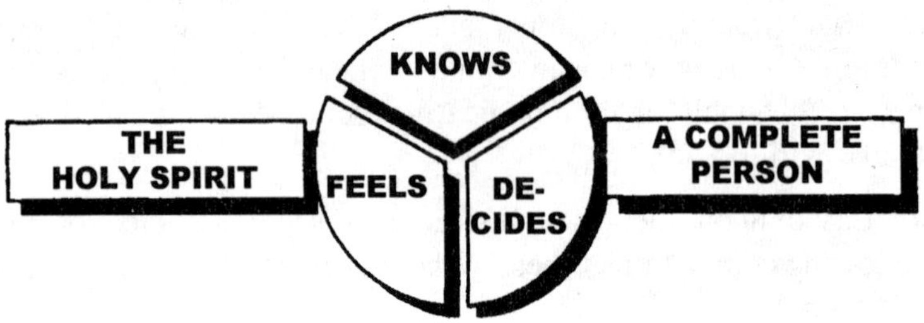

In practical terms, the Spirit's knowledge of the will of God and the needs of people makes it possible for Him to serve as our effective Counselor. This fact is well illustrated in the book of Acts, when the early church assembled in Jerusalem to find solutions for certain problems. In the face of a crisis that could have destroyed the unity of the church, the apostles and elders found a source of comfort and direction in the Holy Spirit (see chapter 15). The Spirit's presence brought about the compromise that was needed, and the apostles were able to write, "It seemed good to the Holy Spirit and to us" (Acts 15:28). Here the wisdom of the Holy Spirit and His divine knowledge provided a solution for the church that satisfied Jews, encouraged Gentiles, and caused the gospel to spread even more effectively.

A person, then, is one who can know *and* be known. As we have seen, the Holy Spirit possesses both of these qualities. He knows you and me better than anyone else can, and He is knowable. How well you will get to know Him will depend on how much you learn about Him from your daily fellowship. He may be treated as a casual acquaintance, or as a very intimate friend. Many say honestly, "I know Him," that is, as a casual acquaintance. Far fewer know Him as an intimate friend. Do you want to know Him better? The more time you spend with Him, the better you will know Him.

2 Complete this sentence: The ability to *know* is a .... characteristic of the Holy Spirit.

3 Based upon Romans 8:27 and 1 Corinthians 2:10-11, choose the best completion for this statement: The Holy Spirit is able to minister to our needs in accordance with God's will because He knows

a) the needs of the people of God.
b) the will of God for His people.
c) the things that people want.
d) all of the above: a), b), and c).
e) the things mentioned in both a) and b) above.

4 How does this Scripture reveal a personal quality of the Holy Spirit: "It seemed good to the Holy Spirit and us"?

....

....

The Ability to Feel

Objective 3. *State what given Scriptures reveal about the Holy Spirit's ability to feel.*

A second quality of personality is the *emotional quality,* or the ability to *feel.* Feelings include the ability to love and to suffer grief, pain, and hurt (including anger). We shall see from Bible accounts that the Holy Spirit has the capacity to feel all these things as He works among us.

Love, like knowledge, is expressed on a person-to-person basis. It needs an object. You must be a person to express love, and the expression of your love would be meaningless if it were not expressed toward another person.

The apostle Paul says, "God has poured out His love into our hearts by the Holy Spirit" (Romans 5:5). And in another place he talks about "the love of the Spirit" (Romans 15:30).

The Holy Spirit is a Person who can be loved, who can love us, and who can love others through us.

A LOVE RELATIONSHIP!

During my college days I had the tendency to overwork the word *love.* I spoke of loving good books and loving good food and loving music. My English teacher objected. Every time I said I loved something, she corrected me. I can still hear her voice, "My brother, you cannot love these things. You can only love a person. Love must be expressed to someone who can respond to it." Her point was simply that love is a communication of one's feelings. To be truly meaningful, this communication must be received by one who can interpret and appreciate the intent of this message and respond to it as well.

Because He is a complete Person, the Holy Spirit can and does express God's love. The love of the Spirit is evident in His earliest dealings with the family of man. In the days of Noah, wickedness was so widespread that the Holy Spirit was "grieved" and He was pained. As a result, God said, "My Spirit will not contend with man forever" (Genesis 6:3). The Spirit can be grieved by people's sin and rebellion because He is capable of feeling. In this case, His love was rejected.

Many people have not responded to the Holy Spirit's love, and His response to their treatment, as we shall see, is another indication of His personal, emotional capacities. He can be the object of personal mistreatment. Paul contrasts the actions of the nonbelievers with those who have come to know Christ. Nonbelievers are not under the control of the Spirit; they are controlled by their sinful natures. In contrast, believers are in the process of change, and the Spirit is in control of their lives. The degree to which the believer yields his life to the Spirit's control appears to determine the progress he makes in putting on the new self and becoming like Christ (compare Romans 8:5-15 with Ephesians 4:17-32). However, if after a time the new believer does not respond to the Spirit's control and continues to demonstrate behaviors characteristic of his old life, the Spirit may indeed be grieved (Ephesians 4:30).

Do you remember how you felt when someone you loved caused you grief or pain? That is how the Holy Spirit feels when we grieve Him.

5 Find these references, and list the personal mistreatment of the Holy Spirit that is mentioned in each. The Holy Spirit may be:

a Acts 5:3 ....

b Acts 7:51 ....

c Hebrews 10:29 ....

d Luke 12:10 ....

e Matthew 12:31-32 ....

6 Read Ephesians 4:25-32 and 5:1-7. Ask yourself: "Am I guilty of grieving the Holy Spirit by doing any of these things which are wrong, or by not responding appropriately to His control?" Make a list of areas where you feel you need to change your attitude or behavior. Write this list in your notebook.

The Ability to Choose

Objective 4. *Select from given Scriptures ways the Holy Spirit exercises His sovereign will in our behalf.*

Another important quality of personality is the ability to decide. Man, who was made in the image of his Creator, is the only created being with the ability to make moral decisions—decisions that affect his eternal destiny. A person can exercise free will. As we shall see in Lesson 2, one of the divine characteristics of the Holy Spirit is His sovereignty, or ability to exercise supreme power or will. The book of Acts shows the will of the Holy Spirit in action.

The commissioning of Barnabas and Saul is a good example of how the Holy Spirit works as a Person with the ability to make choices. Read Acts 13:1-4. Barnabas and Saul could not doubt that the Holy Spirit was a Person—He had called them and then He publicly singled them out for the work He had chosen them to do. His very personal message to them revealed that He was more than just a divine power coming upon them to anoint them for the job God wanted them to do. He was and is a divine Person who selects whomever He chooses according to His own sovereign will.

7 Read the following Scriptures from Romans 8 and complete each sentence to show how the Spirit exercises His sovereign will.

a Romans 8:5 teaches us that the Holy Spirit has ....

b Romans 8:9 shows that the Spirit exercises .... over our lives.

c Romans 8:26 demonstrates that the Spirit .... for us.

This truth is not new if you are familiar with the gifts of the Spirit. Paul teaches that the Holy Spirit distributes His gifts among the members of the church as He *wills* (1 Corinthians 12:7-11). In other words, the Holy Spirit *chooses* the individuals through whom the gifts of the Spirit operate This deliberate selection is the personal act of the Holy Spirit. Each time a gift of the Spirit is manifested, it is an expression of the personality of the Holy Spirit.

8 The following statements deal with evidences of the personality of the Holy spirit. If a statement is TRUE, circle the letter preceding the statement.

a The Holy Spirit is a living being with qualities of personality.

b The essential qualities of personality, as presented in this lesson, are the abilities to know, feel, and decide.

c The fact that the Holy Spirit does not have a physical body keeps Him from being a complete Person.

d The Holy Spirit demonstrates the emotional characteristics of personality.

e The Holy Spirit's capacity to feel is expressed both in His feelings for us, and in His response to our feelings for Him.

f Our relationship with the Holy Spirit is a person-to-Person relationship.

g The Holy Spirit distributes His gifts in the church according to the choices of the receiving members.

h We see in 1 Corinthians 2:10-11 that the quality of *knowing* is a personal quality of the Spirit of God as well as the spirit of man.

HIS PERSONAL OFFICES

Objective 5. *Recognize examples of ways the Holy Spirit functions as Teacher, Administrator and Comforter.*

Can you think of an office that is set up without a plan for having it filled by a person? Offices are always held by persons. Because He is a Person, the Holy Spirit can function as a Teacher, an Administrator, and a Comforter.

The Office of Teacher

There were many things Jesus desired to teach His disciples, but they were not yet ready to receive them. Therefore He promised to send them another Teacher.

Students of the Scriptures learn that the Bible would not have a true spiritual impact if it were not for the personal teaching ministry of the Holy Spirit. He illuminates its truths and applies its lessons to everyday life.

In His teaching concerning the coming ministry of the Holy Spirit, Jesus said, "The Counselor... will teach you all things and will remind you of everything I have said to you" (John 14:26). Moreover, Jesus said of the Spirit, "He will testify about me" (John 15:26). Finally, Jesus concluded His message with a further description of the Spirit's activities in John 16:13-14:

> He will guide you into all truth... and he will tell you what is yet to come. He will bring glory to me by taking from what is mine and making it known to you.

We can expect the Holy Spirit to illuminate the Word of God, bringing clarification to us in the application of Christ's words to our daily lives. He will quicken our memories to recall Christ's words of encouragement in times of crisis (Mark 13:11). Moreover, He will lead us toward spiritual maturity, by leading us into all truth. Finally, He will reveal the course of the future to us and help us to respond appropriately with living that will glorify Christ (Titus 2:11-14).

Sometimes the relationship between a teacher and a student becomes almost as close as that between family members. I have had students introduce me to their parents or friends. When they say, "This is my teacher," their expression shows a special kind of closeness. How much more this is true in the One-to-one teaching relationship with the Holy Spirit. My Teacher, the Holy Spirit, is a complete Person who has a personal relationship with *me.*

9 When the Scriptures say that the Holy Spirit will teach us all things, this may be interpreted to mean that

a) we need no schooling except that which we receive from the Holy Spirit.
b) when we receive the Holy Spirit, we understand all things.
c) the Holy Spirit guides us as we study God's Word and makes its truth clear to us.

The Office of Administrator

Although the book of Acts is called the *Acts of the Apostles,* a more accurate title would be the *Acts of the Holy Spirit.* When the Holy Spirit came on the Day of Pentecost, He became the *superintendent* or director of the church. The book of Acts presents the Holy Spirit as the officer in charge of all of the activities of the early church. What were some of His administrative activities?

The Holy Spirit was instrumental in Philip's ministry to a lone Ethiopian eunuch traveling across the desert. He *commanded* Philip to join the eunuch's chariot and witness to him (Acts 8:26-40).

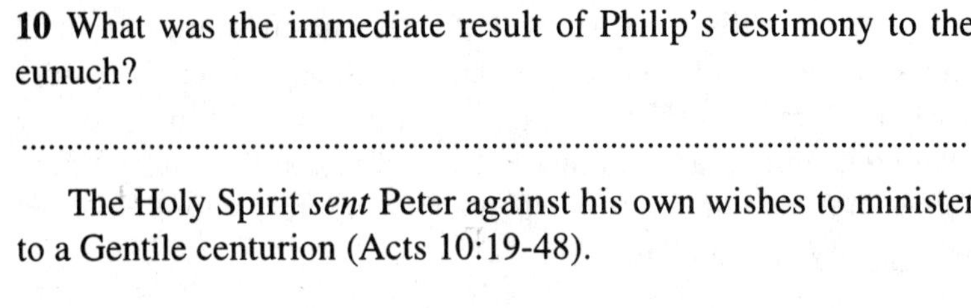

10 What was the immediate result of Philip's testimony to the eunuch?

....

The Holy Spirit *sent* Peter against his own wishes to minister to a Gentile centurion (Acts 10:19-48).

11 What was the primary or immediate result of Peter's ministry to the centurion and all those who heard the message in his home?

....

The Holy Spirit *separated* Barnabas and Saul from their ministry at Antioch and commissioned them for missionary service (Acts 13:1-3). He also brought unity to the council at Jerusalem so that the gospel could be proclaimed effectively to both Jews and Gentiles (Acts 15), giving the gospel message a universal appeal.

When Paul tried to enter Asia and preach the gospel, he was *forbidden* by the Holy Spirit who *would not allow* him to go (Acts 16:6-7). If you will read further, you will see that the Holy Spirit had another plan for Paul at that particular time.

Paul publicly acknowledged the administration of the Holy Spirit when He reminded the Ephesian elders that it was the Holy Spirit who had *appointed* them and placed the church under their care (Acts 20:28). All of these administrative functions of the Holy Spirit confirm that He is a complete Person who was sent by Christ to direct the affairs of His church.

12 Based upon the foregoing discussion, choose the best answer to the following question. What caused Philip, Paul, and Peter to obey the Holy Spirit's direction in the above situations?

a) They had a person-to-Person relationship with Him, and they trusted Him.
b) They were forced to obey Him.
c) They knew what the results would be.

Office of Comforter

When Jesus was leaving the world to return to heaven, His disciples were distressed. They were helpless without Him, so He told them, "I will ask the Father, and he will give you another Counselor to be with you forever" (John 14:16). This title comes from the Greek word *Paraclete* and is usually translated into English as comforter or *helper* or *counselor.* Greek scholars have pointed out that the word translated *another* means "another of the same kind." The Holy Spirit would be a Person *distinct* from Christ, but He would be "of the *same* kind" as Christ, a complete and perfect person.

Christ promised a Person! He did not promise only comfort, and help, and counsel—He promised a *Comforter, a Helper,* and *a Counselor!*

13 Read John 14:15-18, 26; 15:26; 16:12-15 and complete the following statements.

a Jesus promised His disciples that He would not leave them as

....,

that is, helpless, forlorn, and alone.

b Jesus promised that the Father would send another ....

....

to take His place forever.

c The ministry of the Holy Spirit would be to ....

....

d Jesus said that when this *other* Comforter came, He would guide His own into .... and bring glory to ....

14 Match each example left) to the function of the Holy Spirit it describes (right

.... **a**	Reminds us of Jesus' words, leads us into truth, makes the Word clear to us	1) Teacher
.... **b**	Takes the place of another as our Helper, Counselor, and trusted Friend	2) Administrator
.... **c**	Provides leadership and direction for the activities of the church	3) Comforter

HIS PERSONAL DESIGNATIONS

Objective 6. *Give examples of personal designations of the Holy Spirit.*

In addition to the qualities and offices which show the personality of the Holy Spirit, the Bible assigns Him personal names and uses personal pronouns to refer to Him.

The name *Holy Spirit* appears over 90 times in the Bible. It is His personal name and sets forth His own essential character.

Now we will see that Jesus revealed the personality of the Holy Spirit. We will also note that the Holy Spirit designates Himself as a Person.

Revealed by Jesus

Let's look more closely at the promise of Jesus when He speaks of the coming of the Holy Spirit (John 14, 15, and 16). Jesus clearly and unmistakably assigns personality to the Holy Spirit through the use of a personal name and by the personal pronouns He uses.

> "I will ask the Father and he will give you another Counselor to be with you forever" (John 14:16). "When the *Counselor* comes . . . *he* will testify about me" (John 15:26). "But when *he,* the Spirit of truth, comes, *he* will

guide you into all truth. *He* will not speak on *his* own; *he* will speak only what *he* hears, and *he* will tell you what is yet to come" (John 16:13).

It is obvious in these passages that Jesus wanted His disciples to know that He was sending a *Person* to take His place. Three times He used the personal designation *Counselor,* or *Comforter.* Then seven times in one short verse He used the personal masculine pronoun *he* to refer to the Holy Spirit. He might easily have omitted some of these pronouns or used the neuter designation, *spirit,* but he repeated the personal designations over and over. I think Jesus wanted to emphasize that the Holy Spirit is a *Person,* and He acts as a person.

Revealed by Himself

Has it occurred to you yet that all of these Bible statements were inspired by the Holy Spirit (2 Peter 1 :20-21)? This means that behind all that is being said, the Holy Spirit, who is the Agent of revelation, reveals that He is a complete Person. Moreover, He gives further evidence of His personality as He refers to His activity in personal terms.

One reference we have already used says it clearly and directly. It is a statement of the Holy Spirit Himself: "... the Holy Spirit said, 'Set apart for me Barnabas and Saul for the work to which *I* have called them'," (Acts 13:2).

Revealed by the Apostle Paul

In his remarkable section on *Life Through the Spirit* in Romans 8, verses 1 through 27, Paul uses the personal masculine pronoun *Himself* (vs. 16, 26) to refer to the Holy Spirit. He did not use the neuter designation itself, but instead he used the designation which indicates that the One who verifies our sonship and intercedes for us is a *Person.* The apostle wanted us to understand that the One who controls our minds, produces life in us, makes our relationship with Christ real, and helps us in prayer has the characteristics of personality which make it possible for us to have this personal relationship with Him.

15 Match each statement (left) with the person whom it describes (right).

.... **a**	Spoke of the coming *Comforter* and referred to Him seven times by the personal pronoun *he*	1) Jesus 2) The Holy Spirit
.... **b**	Said, "Set apart for me Barnabas and Saul for the work which I have called them to do"	
.... **c**	Said, "When the *Counselor* comes ... *he* will testify about me"	

16 List the personal designations of the Holy Spirit discussed here which could only be given to a *person.*

....

OUR PERSONAL RELATIONSHIP

Objective 7. *Select a correct explanation of the relationship we have with the Holy Spirit when we know Him as a Person.*

There are a number of reasons why it is important for us to know the Holy Spirit as a complete Person. One of them is that such knowledge deepens our relationship with Him.

Many of the problems the church experiences in the operation of spiritual gifts could be avoided if we would seek to know the Person of the Holy Spirit *before* we desire to receive and exercise His gifts. The knowledge of the Person of the Holy Spirit should bring a deep desire to please Him and be used by Him. This knowledge should in no way limit the operation of the spiritual gifts; indeed, it need not.

A Right Relationship

You have reviewed evidence which shows that the Holy Spirit is a *knowing* Person. This knowledge should give you a solid basis for sharing your problems with Him and letting Him show you how to solve them.

You have also considered evidence that He is an *emotional* being. This evidence gives you insights into the things He desires. You should no longer think of using Him to fulfill your desires; rather, you should allow Him to use you to fulfill His desires. a loving, sensitive being, who can be grieved by your misconduct. Pleasing yourself should not then be as important as pleasing Him.

Finally, you have evaluated evidence which shows that He is capable of choosing and deciding. His knowledge is infinite and He knows what is best for you. Moreover, He has *chosen* you and empowered you to be His witness. I trust you will greatly value His gifts. But more than the gifts, may you ever honor and value the Giver.

A Meaningful Relationship

Another very important value in recognizing the Holy Spirit as a Person is that *relationship* means more to the believer than experience. Knowing the power of the Holy Spirit brings some exciting experiences, but one enters a truly meaningful relationship with Him only when he comes to know Him as a Person. Such a relationship is a developing thing. It brings with it not only the knowledge of one's spiritual privileges but also the knowledge of his responsibilities. Paul refers to the progressive nature of this relationship in 2 Corinthians 3:18: "And we, who with unveiled faces all reflect the Lord's glory, are being transformed into his likeness with ever-increasing glory."

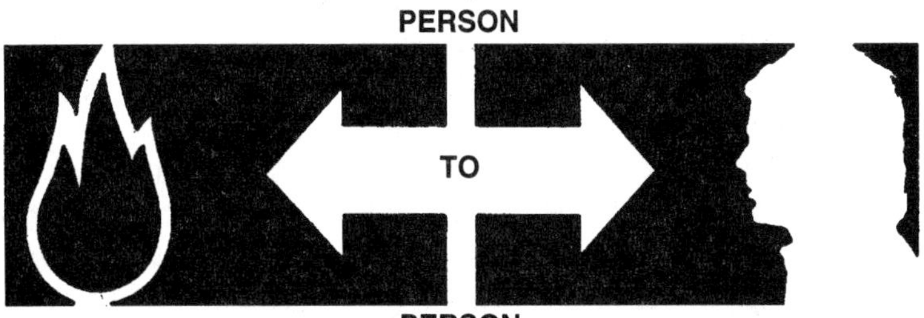

The way one looks at the baptism in the Holy Spirit (Acts 2:4) is a good illustration of this. If he is *experience oriented,* he will see the baptism as an end in itself. When he has received *it*, he feels he has achieved his goal. if, on the other hand, he views the baptism in the Holy Spirit as involving the Person of the Holy Spirit, he recognizes that each day is filled with potential for the development of this relationship. This relationship can be expanded continually as long as he lives and desires to be filled with the Spirit (Ephesians 5:18). Remember: Jesus promised that the Holy Spirit would come to be with us forever (John 14:16).

If you have been experience oriented, now is a good time to recognize your person-to-Person relationship with the Holy Spirit. He wants you to be so filled with His presence that your chief desire will be to please Him and do His will.

17 Examine your own relationship with the Holy Spirit by studying these examples. Place a 1) in front of the statements which are *relationship oriented* and a 2) in front of those that are *experience oriented.*

. . . . **a** "When I receive the baptism in the Holy Spirit, I feel I will have reached the limit of my spiritual growth."

. . . . **b** "Since I have received the Holy Spirit, I have grown spiritually. Each day brings a sweeter and richer fellowship with the Lord."

. . . . **c** "I can hardly wait for the revival meeting next week, because I want a blessing. While I tend to get discouraged between special meetings and give place to the old self, when the Spirit moves I forget everything but my blessing."

. . . . **d** "The Spirit's presence in my life is the source of my strength. Since He came into my life in baptismal fullness, I've matured in terms of spiritual value. Now my goal is to please Him."

18 Based upon the discussion in this section of the lesson, which statements best explain the relationship we have with the Holy Spirit when we know Him as a Person? If we know Him as a Person who should be in control of our lives, we will tend to be

a) more interested in the spiritual experiences we have and how they make us feel.
b) concerned about pleasing Him and about becoming more Spirit-controlled and less controlled by the sinful nature every day.
c) more aware of His presence in our lives as our source of help and strength.
d) better able to choose the spiritual gifts we want to have.

self-test

After you have reviewed the lesson, take this self-test. Then check your answers with those we have given at the back of this study guide. Review any items answered incorrectly.

TRUE-FALSE. If the statement is TRUE, write **T** in the blank space. If it is FALSE, write **F**.

. . . . **1** The Holy Spirit is said to have personality because He has influence and power.

. . . . **2** Three qualities of personality which the Holy Spirit possesses are the ability to know, to feel, and to choose.

. . . . **3** The Holy Spirit can and does express the love of God.

. . . . **4** The ability to choose is an expression of that part of the personality which is called the will.

. . . . **5** The Holy Spirit functions primarily in the office of judge.

. . . . **6** Three important offices of the Holy Spirit are Teacher, Administrator, and Comforter.

. . . . **7** Because a thing has a name it is considered a personality.

. . . . **8** Scripture refers to the Holy Spirit by impersonal designations.

. . . . **9** Jesus referred to the Holy Spirit as a Person, using a personal name and personal pronouns as He spoke.

COMPLETION. Fill in the blanks with one of these words to complete the statements:

complete	relationship	experience
desires	maturity	problems

10 If you recognize the Holy Spirit as a Person, you can share your .... with Him and let Him show you how to solve them.

11 When you come to see the Holy Spirit as an emotional being, you should also understand that He has ...., and you should seek to please Him, and not yourself.

12 People who are .... oriented tend to see the baptism in the Holy Spirit as an end in itself.

13 Those who view the baptism in the Holy Spirit as involving a Person tend to be .... oriented.

14 If one truly values the potential of the baptism in the Holy Spirit, he should begin a relationship that will produce progressive Christian..

15 When we say that the Holy Spirit is a .... Person, we mean He possesses all of the qualities which make it possible for us to have a personal relationship with Him.

SHORT ANSWER. Answer each question as briefly as possible.

16 List the three personal qualities of the Holy Spirit we have studied in this lesson.

17 Explain how the love relationship with the Holy Spirit works.

....

....

18 Name three ways the Holy Spirit can be mistreated which reveal that He has feelings.

....

answers to study questions

The answers to your study exercises are not given in the usual order, so that you will not see the answer to your next question ahead of time. Look for the number you need, and try not to look ahead.

10 The eunuch received the message, was baptized, and went on his way rejoicing.

1 b) He has the essential qualities of personality.

11 They accepted the message, were filled with the Holy Spirit, and were baptized.

2 personal

12 a) They had a person-to-Person relationship with Him, and they trusted Him.

3 e) the things mentioned in a) and b) above.

13 **a** orphans (comfortless).
b Counselor, Comforter, or Helper.
c teach and remind of what Jesus said.
d all truth, Jesus.

4 It reveals that He had the knowledge to provide a solution, and that He was able to communicate that knowledge to the apostles.

14 **a** 1) Teacher.
b 3) Comforter.
c 2) Administrator.

5 The Holy Spirit may be:
a lied to.
b resisted.
c insulted.
d blasphemed (this action is the most serious of all).
e spoken and sinned against.

15 a 1) Jesus.
b 2) The Holy Spirit.
c 1) Jesus.

6 Your Answer.

16 Holy Spirit (personal name), Comforter, he, me, I

7 a wants or desires.
b control
c intercedes

17 a 2) Experience oriented
b 1) Relationship oriented
c 2) Experience oriented
d 1) Relationship oriented

8 a True
b True
c False
d True
e True
f True
g False
h True

18 b) concerned about pleasing Him.
c) more aware of His presence.

9 c) the Holy Spirit guides us as we study God's Word and makes its truth clear to us.

LESSON 2

A DIVINE PERSON

The Holy Spirit is a member of the Godhead, coequal with God the Father and God the Son. Throughout Scripture, beginning with the Creation and continuing through the final chapter of Revelation, we see the Holy Spirit acting with the other members of the Trinity in the course of human history. But the work of the Spirit in the lives of men entered a new phase after ascension of Christ to the right hand of the Father (Acts 1:1-9).

We who have limited knowledge cannot fully comprehend the concept of the Trinity—one God, but three distinct Persons who act in perfect unity and cooperation. In the Old Testament, God, the Father, spoke through a few selected people by His Spirit. Jesus, the Son, was God Incarnate, God made flesh, revealing the Father to us in His earthly ministry. God, the Holy Spirit, was sent by the Father and the Son to work through Christ's body, the church.

In this lesson we will see that the Holy Spirit is a *divine* Person, the third member of the Trinity, worthy of our honor and obedience. He is a divine Person who longs to minister in our lives daily, conforming us into the image of the Son and leading us into service for Him. The Holy Spirit never draws attention to Himself; He always points us to our Savior, Jesus Christ. Have you allowed this divine Person to dwell within *you*? Is He *your* Comforter, *your* Companion, *your* Guide? Let Him speak to your heart as you study this lesson.

lesson outline

Divine Association
Divine Attributes
Divine Acclamation
Divine Sufficiency

lesson objectives

When you finish this lesson you should be able to:

- Give scriptural evidence of the deity of the Holy Spirit based on divine association, divine attributes, and divine acclamation.
- Apply to your own life the implications of the deity of the Holy Spirit as seen in His sufficiency for every human need.

learning activities

1. Study the lesson in the manner described in the learning activities for Lesson 1. Read the lesson content, find and read all Scripture texts given, and answer the study questions.
2. Look in the glossary for definitions of any key words you do not know. If there are other words you do not understand, find the definitions for them in your dictionary.
3. Take the self-test and check your answers with those given at the back of this study guide.

key words

acclamation	nurture	sovereign
attributes	omnipotent	sufficiency
benediction	omnipresent	transformed
deity	omniscient	Trinity
Incarnate	purity	Triune
manifestation		

lesson development

DIVINE ASSOCIATION

Objective 1. *Choose a definition of the Holy Spirit which reflects His association with God the Father and God the Son, based on given Scriptures.*

Any reason for believing in the deity of the Father or the Son may be equally applied to the Holy Spirit. The apostle Peter states categorically that sin against the Holy Spirit is sin against God (Acts 5:3-4). Here the Holy Spirit's deity is unmistakably asserted. Although He is a distinct Person, the Holy Spirit's associations with the other members of the Trinity are so close that He has been called, at different times, "the Spirit of your Father" (Matthew 10:20) and "the Spirit of Christ" (Romans 8:9).

There is much scriptural evidence which reveals to us that the Holy Spirit is associated with the other members of the Godhead as a distinct, divine Person, on the same level as the Father and the Son, and in perfect unity with them. Let us look at some of the scriptural evidence.

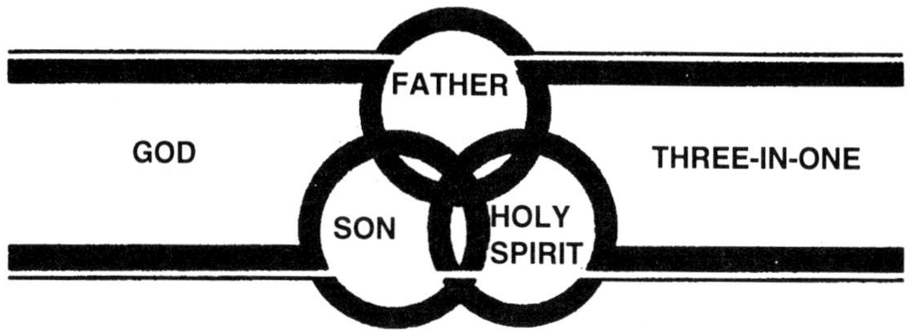

The Baptismal Formula

Jesus Himself gave equal recognition to the Holy Spirit when He gave this command to His disciples:

Therefore go and make disciples of all nations, baptizing them in the name of the Father and of the Son and of the Holy Spirit, and teaching them to obey everything I have commanded you (Matthew 28:19-20).

Since that time, many believers have followed this formula and have been baptized in the name of the Father, the Son, and the Holy Spirit—the Triune God. Note that in this command Jesus did not use the plural "in the *names* of." This is further evidence of the unity in the Trinity.

This association is clearly seen in the baptism of Jesus by John the Baptist.

1 Read John 1:25-34 and Luke 3:15-16, 21-22, and answer these questions:

a In what two ways is the Holy Spirit associated with the baptism of Jesus?

....

....

b What verse indicates that God the Father was also associated with the baptism of Jesus?

....

The Apostolic Benediction

One of the best loved and most often quoted benedictions of the church is another testimony of the Scriptures to the deity of the Holy Spirit. In 2 Corinthians 13:14 the apostle Paul closes his second letter to the Corinthian believers with these words:

> May the grace of the Lord Jesus Christ, and the love of God, and the fellowship of the Holy Spirit be with you all.

This Scripture not only associates the Holy Spirit with the Father and the Son in name, but also in ministry. The three attributes given to the three Persons in the Trinity in this Scripture might well remind us of the most significant way each of them has touched our lives: the undying love of the Father, who loved us so much that He gave us His own beloved Son; the never-falling grace of our Savior Jesus Christ, who died for us while we were yet sinners; and the enduring companionship of our divine Friend, the Holy Spirit. When we accept the love, the grace, and the fellowship of our Triune God, we have everything that we need to sustain spiritual life and maintain an acceptable relationship to God.

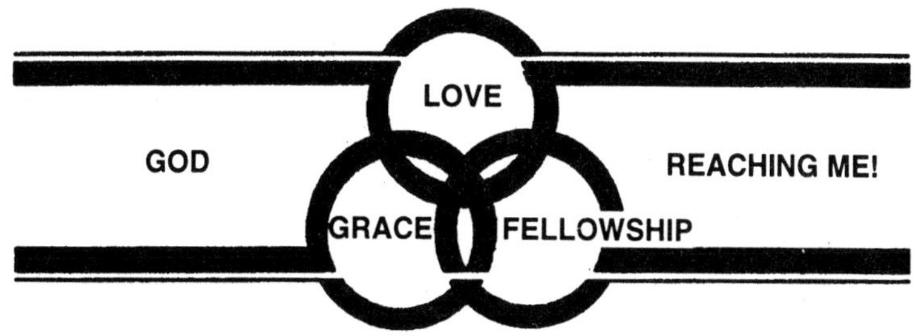

Other Scripture Accounts

2 Read Genesis 1:1-2 and 26. In what ways is the Holy Spirit associated with the Creation account in these verses? What do the plural pronouns *us* and *our* in verse 26 suggest?

....

....

3 Read Matthew 1:18-19. How was the Holy Spirit associated with the birth of Christ?

....

....

4 Read Isaiah 61:1-2 and Luke 4:14-21. How is the Holy Spirit associated with Christ's earthly ministry?

....

....

If you have a Bible concordance, you would be enriched if you search for other Scriptures which clearly associate the Holy Spirit with God the Father and God the Son. Make a list of the Scriptures you find and the significance of each one.

5 Based upon the scriptural evidence we have considered, select the best completion for this statement: The baptismal formula, the apostolic benediction, the Creation account, and the birth of Jesus are among the important Scriptures which reveal to us that the Holy Spirit is

a) God, with higher power than the Father or the Son.
b) a member of the Triune Godhead, coequal to the Father and Son and in perfect unity with them.
c) God, with lesser power than the Father or the Son.
d) not God, but a spiritual force used by God to carry out His will.

DIVINE ATTRIBUTES

Objective 2. *Complete a chart on the attributes of God which gives scriptural evidence of the deity of the Holy Spirit.*

Another evidence of the deity of the Holy Spirit is that He possesses attributes which only God can posses. In Lesson 1 we introduced some of the divine qualities which are true of the Holy Spirit. In addition to God's personal qualities mentioned there, Scripture teaches us that God alone is the source and giver of life (Acts 17:24-25).

Interestingly, several Scriptures attribute these life-giving characteristics to the Holy Spirit also. In fact, one of the tides of the Holy Spirit is "Spirit of Life." The apostle Paul said explicitly that the Spirit raised Jesus from the dead (Romans 8:11), and Jesus affirmed the same, indicating that it is the Spirit who gives life (John 6:63). In his second letter to the Corinthian church, the apostle Paul proclaimed, "the Spirit gives life" (2 Corinthians 3:6). The apostle Peter declared that Jesus "was put to death in the body but made alive by the Spirit" (1 Peter 3:18).

6 Read the Scriptures (right) and match each Scripture or set of Scriptures with the attribute of God to which it refers (left).

. . . . **a** Personality	1) John 4:24
. . . . **b** Eternal	2) Corinthians 8:6
. . . . **c** Triune	3) Genesis 2:18; Isaiah 1:14; 55:8
. . . . **d** Spirit	4) John 14:23-26
. . . . **e** Unchanging	5) Psalm 90:1-2
. . . . **f** One God	6) Psalm 33:11; 102:25-27; Malachi 3:6

Now let's look at some of the attributes of God which the Holy Spirit shares with the Father and the Son, as revealed in Scripture.

He Is Holy

The personal name of the third person of the Trinity which most often appears in the Bible is *Holy* Spirit. Since God alone possesses the quality of absolute holiness or purity, His name affirms His deity. The apostle Paul emphasized His attribute of absolute holiness when he called Him the "Spirit of holiness" (Romans 1:4). Some Bible scholars suggest that the "Holy, holy, holy" of Isaiah 6:3 and Revelation 4:8 is a recognition of the Triune nature of God.

He Is Eternal

In Hebrews 9:14, the Holy Spirit is called the *eternal* spirit. The word *eternal* in this Scripture is the same word used to describe the eternal nature of God the Father and God the Son in other Scriptures. In Contrast to the *eternal* Spirit, Paul says that *all* other things visible and invisible (which would seem to include all other Spirits) were created at a point in time (Colossians 1:15-16). The Holy Spirit, however, is declared to be eternally self-existent. He has no beginning and will have no ending. He always was, He is, and He always will be. His eternal nature is a proof of His divinity.

He Is Sovereign

In Lesson 1 we saw that one element of the Holy Spirit's personality is His *will.* His will, which is perfect, is a manifestation of His deity.

Jesus likened the Spirit to the wind "that blows wherever it pleases" (John 3:8). Since God alone can do as He pleases, we see further evidence of the Spirit's deity. In 1 Corinthians 12, Paul refers to the Holy Spirit's sovereign nature in his treatment of spiritual gifts. The Spirit, he notes, dispenses spiritual gifts selectively: to one He gives this gift and to another that gift. He thus exercises the divine prerogative of sovereignty, which Paul clearly describes. "He gives them to each man, just as he determines" (1 Corinthians 12:11).

The word *sovereign* means "possessed of supreme power." There is no power higher than God's power. The Holy Spirit's sovereign power is the supreme power which God alone possesses. The fact that He created us with a will and a power to make choices is something that He *chose* to do. He wanted us to exercise our will in making a choice to serve Him, rather than forcing us to serve him. It is only because of His sovereign will that our own will can function.

7 Read Acts 13:2 and 1 Corinthians 2:4; then complete these statements:

a In Acts 13:2, the Holy Spirit's sovereign will is seen in his .... to the prophets and teachers at Antioch and in the .... of Barnabas and Saul.

b In 1 Corinthians 2:4, the power of the Spirit in Paul's life is seen to be greater than ....

He Is Omnipresent

The word *omnipresent* means "everywhere present." The psalmist David asked of God, "Where can I go from your Spirit?... If you go up to the heavens, you are there; if I make my bed in the depths, you are there" (Psalm 139:7-8). There is no place to hide from the Holy Spirit. He is at all times everywhere present.

No other spirit can claim this ability. Even Satan is a created being who is limited to one place at a time. He must depend on other fallen angels to help him carry out his evil work.

The divine Spirit of God does not have to depend on an organization of lesser spirits to administrate the redemptive program of God. He is personally present to strive with every sinner (John 16:7-11) and comfort every saint (John 16:13; 14:16-17). He was sent by the Father and the Son to abide in the heart of every believer and to fill every believer with His divine power (Acts 1:8). Today we are living in the "last days" of which the prophet Joel spoke, and the Holy Spirit has been "poured out" upon every believer who will receive Him (See Acts 2:16-18.) Have you experienced the divine presence of the Holy Spirit working in your life?

He Is Omniscient

Nothing is hidden from the Holy Spirit—He is omniscient (all knowing). All that has happened from the beginning of time and before is known by the Holy Spirit. Everything that is happening everywhere at the present time and all that will ever happen in the future is known in perfect detail by Him. The apostle Paul revealed the omniscience of the Holy Spirit in his letter to the Corinthians:

> However, as it is written: "No eye has seen, no ear has heard, no mind has conceived what God has prepared for those who love him"—but God has revealed it to us by his Spirit. The Spirit searches all things, even the deep things of God. For who among men knows the thoughts of a man except the man's spirit within him? In the same

way no one knows the thoughts of God except the Spirit of God (1 Corinthians 2:9-11).

He Is Omnipotent

The Holy Spirit is "all powerful." He is called "The power of the Most High" (Luke 1:35). In other words, the power of the Holy Spirit is the power of God. His power is unlimited—"All things are possible with God" (Mark 10:27).

The Holy Spirit's power is imparted to chosen instruments of God throughout Scripture—for example, David (1 Samuel 16:13) and Micah (Micah 3:8); the disciples (John 20:19-23); and upon all who will receive (Acts 1 :8).

In Zechariah 4:6 the word of the Lord came to Zerubbabel: "'Not by might nor by power, but by my Spirit, says the Lord Almighty.'" This might be paraphrased "Not by human might nor by human power, but by the power of my Spirit, says the Lord Almighty." Stanley M. Horton emphasizes that "'By my Spirit' is a fundamental principle that all who are fellow laborers with the Lord must keep in mind" (Horton, 1976, pp. 74-75). This Scripture is an affirmation of the omnipotence of the Holy Spirit.

8 Match each attribute (right) with its description (left). Write the number of your choice in each blank space.

. . . . **a** Absolute purity

. . . . **b** Having no beginning and no end; existing forever

. . . . **c** Possessed of the highest power over all that exists; able to do as He wills

. . . . **d** All knowing

. . . . **e** Present everywhere

. . . . **f** All powerful

1) Sovereign
2) Omniscient
3) Holy
4) Omnipotent
5) Eternal
6) Omnipresent

9 Read the Scriptures below which provide evidence of the deity of God as revealed in the Father and the Son. Then complete the chart by supplying scriptural proofs of the deity of the Holy Spirit according to His divine attributes.

Attributes of God	Father	Son	Holy Spirit
a Holiness	Psalm 22:3 Exodus 19:12-25	Acts 3:14	
b Eternality	Psalm 90:2 Psalm 102:27	Micah 5:2 John 1:1	
c Sovereignty	Job 42:2	Matthew 28:18 1 Peter 3:22	
d Omnipresence	Psalm 139:7-12	Matthew 18:20 Ephesians 1:22-23	
e Omniscience	Psalm 139:1-6	John 2:24-25 Colossians 2:2-3	
f Omnipotence	Psalm 139:13-19 Matthew 19:26	Luke 7:11-17	

DIVINE ACCLAMATION

Objective 3. *Based on 2 Peter 1:20-21, explain why we can accept statements of individuals recorded in the Bible which acclaim the deity of the Holy Spirit.*

The deity of the Holy Spirit is also confirmed by direct statements of individuals in the Bible who call Him God. Simeon, Peter, and the apostle Paul are examples of men who made such statements.

Simeon's Statement

In Luke's Gospel account we are told that Simeon was a righteous and devout man who lived in Jerusalem. He was a Jew looking for the coming of the Messiah. The Scripture tells us that he received confirmation from the Holy Spirit about this event:

> Now there was a man in Jerusalem called Simeon, who was righteous and devout. He was waiting for the consolation of Israel, and the Holy Spirit was upon him. It had been revealed to him by the Holy Spirit that he would not die before he had seen the Lord's Christ. Moved by the Spirit, he went into the temple courts. When the parents brought in the child Jesus . . . Simeon took him in his arms and praised God, saying: "Sovereign Lord, as you have promised, you now dismiss your servant in peace. For my eyes have seen your salvation" (Luke 2:25-30).

In this passage the Spirit's omniscience is seen in His revelation of the thoughts of God that would otherwise have been unknown or unknowable to Simeon. According to Peter, this prophecy, which originated with God, was communicated by the omnipotent Spirit (2 Peter 1:20-21). Since there is unity in the Godhead, what applies to the one Person applies equally to the others. Hence the deity of the Holy Spirit is once again in evidence.

Peter's Statement

Some of the believers in the early church were selling their properties and bringing the money to the apostles for distribution to the needy (Acts 4:32-36). Among these believers were a husband and wife, Ananias and Sapphira. They, too, sold their property and kept back part of the money they received, but they pretended they were giving all of it to the church. The apostle Peter sensed by the Holy Spirit what they had done.

10 Read Acts 1-4 and complete these statements of Peter to Ananias:

a "Ananias, how is it that Satan has so filled your heart that you have lied to ...."

b "You have not lied to me but to ...."

In this Scripture, Peter indicates that lying to the Holy Spirit is the same as lying to God.

Paul's Statements

In both of his letters to the Corinthian church, the apostle Paul made statements which give further evidence of the deity of the Holy Spirit. The first statement is made in 1 Corinthians 2:4-5: "My message and my preaching were not with wise and persuasive words, but with a demonstration of the Spirit's power, so that your faith might not rest on men's wisdom, but on God's power." Here Paul acclaims the deity of the Holy Spirit, for he dearly equates the Spirit's power with God's power. He gave additional evidence concerning this matter in 1 Corinthians 3:16: "Don't you know that you yourselves are God's temple and that God's Spirit lives in you?" The inference here is that believers are temples of God, indwelt by God the Holy Spirit.

Again, in writing to the Corinthians Paul told them that the veil which kept the Jews from understanding the scriptures could be removed if they turned to the Lord. Then he said these words:

> Now the Lord is the Spirit, and where the Spirit of the Lord is, there is freedom. And we, who with unveiled faces all reflect the Lord's glory, are being transformed into his likeness with ever-increasing glory, which comes from the Lord, who is the Spirit (2 Corinthians 3:17-18).

11 Read 2 Peter 1:20-21 and on the basis of that Scripture explain why the statements of Simeon, Peter, and Paul can be considered further evidence of the deity of the Holy Spirit.

....

....

DIVINE SUFFICIENCY

Objective 4. *Select given words which explain by what means the Holy Spirit is able to provide our needs.*

As we develop in spiritual understanding, it is important for us to examine the scriptural evidence which reveal the deity of the Holy Spirit, as well as divine attributes and place in the Godhead. Without such knowledge, we can neither benefit fully from His daily ministry to us, nor can we give Him the place of glory and honor which is rightfully His. We often miss some important things in life when we lack information. God said through Hosea, the prophet, "my people are destroyed from lack of knowledge" (Hosea 4:6). There was "no acknowledgment of God in the land" (Hosea 4:1). Unless we know who the Holy

Spirit is and what *He can do for us,* and for mankind, we cannot benefit fully from His divine sufficiency.

Many of the things we have learned about the deity of the Holy Spirit have a practical application in our daily lives. There is no lack in His desire or power to meet our needs. Because He is divine, the Holy Spirit is sufficient for *all* of our needs. Let us look at some of the ways He wants to work in our lives. We will briefly summarize them here, as they will be developed more fully in later lessons. Our purpose for this lesson is simply to illustrate that because the Holy Spirit is one of the three Persons in the Godhead, He is fully sufficient to provide for us whatever we need.

He Imparts Spiritual Life

When Nicodemus came to Jesus, he expected to learn from Him as a teacher sent from God. He was surprised when Jesus said that he must be born again. Jesus went on to say, "Unless a man is born of water and the Spirit, he cannot enter the kingdom of God. Flesh gives birth to flesh, but the Spirit gives birth to spirit" (see John 3:5-6).

To be born of the Spirit is to receive the life of God. Without spiritual life, you can never do the things that please God.

Paul tells the Romans of the hopeless struggle he had before he allowed the "Spirit of life" to set him free from the law of sin and death. His confession is familiar to all of us, because his experience is our experience:

> For I have the desire to do what is good, but I cannot carry it out. For what I do is not the good I want to do; no, the evil I do not want to do—this I keep on doing (Romans 7:18-19).

12 The solution to this problem is found in Romans 8:5-9. Read this Scripture and use it as a basis for judging whether the following statements are TRUE or FALSE Circle the letters preceding the TRUE statements.

a If we allow the Holy Spirit to give us spiritual life, we will want things that He wants.

b If we live according to our own nature, without the life-giving help of the Holy Spirit, we will be able to control our evil desires most of the time.

c When the Spirit imparts spiritual life to us and controls our minds, He also gives us peace of mind.

d Without the help of the Holy Spirit it is impossible to please God.

e When the Spirit imparts spiritual life to us, He actually dwells within us and takes control of our lives, freeing us from all responsibility for spiritual life.

13 Here is a list of Scriptures that we studied earlier in this lesson: Acts 17:24-25; Romans 8:11; John 6:63; 2 Corinthians 3:6; 1 Peter 3:18. What is their significance as you apply them to your own needs?

....

....

He Nurtures Holiness

"Without holiness," the Bible says, "no one will see the Lord" (Hebrews 12:14). We have just seen in Romans 8:5-9 that as we surrender our lives to the control of the Holy Spirit, we are enabled to remain spiritually alive and to live uprightly before God. Through the power of the indwelling Spirit we are able to obey the scriptural admonition "to be holy in all we do" (1 Peter 1:14-15). In Romans 6:22 Paul sets forth the new believer's responsibility. Having been set free from sin, he is to become God's slave. One benefit of this servitude is holiness. The apostle indicates that our part in the process is to cooperate with the

Spirit, purifying ourselves from all that would contaminate our spiritual life (compare Romans 8:5-11 with 2 Corinthians 7:1 and Ephesian 8 4:22-24). When we fail in our spiritual obligation (Romans 8:12-14), namely, to keep step with the Spirit (Galatians 5:25), we are disciplined for one primary purpose: ". . . that we may share in His (God's) holiness" (Hebrews 12:10). With the Spirit in control of our lives, we will grow in holiness.

14 Read again Romans 8:5-17. This Scripture passage gives us the key to effective Christian living. What is this key?

....

....

He Gives Power

As you surrender control of your life to the indwelling Holy Spirit, He gives you power:

1. To witness (Acts 1:8)
2. To be an overcomer (1 John 5:4-5)
3. For service (1 Corinthians 12:4-11)
4. To test the spirits and overcome them (1 John 4:1-4)
5. Over fear, anxiety, and trials (2 Timothy 1:7; 2 Corinthians 6:4-10)

Because of the power of the Holy Spirit, you need not live your whole life a slave of fear. He gives you holy boldness to face the battles of life, and He gives you power over evil. The knowledge that the One who is with you is the "Power of the

Most High" (Luke 1:35) will give you the will to resist evil and the faith to believe for victory over the attacks of the evil one (James 4:7; 1 John 4:4). You can have peace and security in any situation you face because you know that the Holy Spirit was sent by Jesus to be your protector and helper (John 14:25-27).

15 (Choose the best answer.) According to the foregoing Scriptures, we conclude that it is possible to live a victorious Christian life without fear because

a) all Christians are promised freedom from the attack of evil spirits.
b) believers recognize that evil spirits are utterly powerless.
c) the Holy Spirit power is infinite, and through faith in His power the believer can conquer fear and live victoriously.

He Provides Companionship

When Jesus came to this earth in human form, His disciples had the privilege of close companionship with Him. This relationship was intended to be a temporary one. It would end 1) when the disciples had learned the lessons of disciple-making and were prepared to continue His ministry and 2) when His redemptive mission was accomplished. As Jesus brought His ministry to a close, He knew that His disciples relied heavily on His presence. He knew they would be like orphans without Him. To prepare them for His departure, that is, to fill the void He would leave, He asked the Father to send the Holy Spirit to take His place:

And I will ask the Father, and he will give you another Counselor to be with you forever (John 14:16). But I tell you the truth: It is for your good that I am going away. Unless I go away, the Counselor will not come to you; but if I go, I will send him to you (John 16:7).

Because God sent His Holy Spirit to abide in our hearts, to be our Counselor and Guide, we never need to feel lonely. The Holy Spirit, who is omnipresent, can be a companion to every believer in the world at the same time. This quality of God enables Him to be with me as I write and with you as you study this lesson. He is ever present to teach us, encourage us, and be our companion in every circumstance. Whereas Jesus could be in only one place at a time, the Holy Spirit is everywhere present. Is it any wonder Jesus said it was for the good of His followers that He go away? In His absence the Counselor lives within each of us to provide the closest possible companionship (1 Corinthians 3:16).

16 Complete each of these sentences with one of these words:

omnipotent	omniscient	life
omnipresent	righteousness	

a The Holy Spirit can give me spiritual life because He is the Spirit of ....

b I can be holy as the Holy Spirit controls my life and imparts to me the .... of God.

c I can receive spiritual power for Christian life and witness because the Holy Spirit is ....

d Because He is .... , the Holy Spirit is my constant companion.

Now that we have discussed the deity of the Holy Spirit and found that He longs to be your Companion and Guide, ask yourself these questions: Have I allowed the Spirit of God to impart spiritual life to me through faith in Christ's sacrifice for me? Is He working in my life to perfect holiness in me, conforming me into the image of Christ? Is the power of the Holy Spirit working through me every day of my life? Is He ever present in my life to give me divine comfort, wisdom, and strength? I hope you have answered *yes* to all of these questions. Welcome Him into your life and allow Him to use you through His divine power!

self-test

TRUE-FALSE If the statement is TRUE, write **T** in the blank space. If the statement is FALSE, write **F**.

.... **1** We call the Holy Spirit the Third Person of the Trinity because He ranks lower than the Father and the Son.

.... **2** The word *Trinity* refers to three Persons who are one God with perfect unity and who arc coequal.

.... **3** One way we know the Holy Spirit is divine is that He possesses the attributes of deity.

.... **4** *Omniscience* refers to the Holy Spirit's power to do anything.

.... **5** In the present day the Holy Spirit's power has been poured out upon a few selected people for a short period of time.

.... **6** Jesus Himself was empowered by the Holy Spirit in His earthly ministry.

.... **7** There are numerous references in Scripture which associate the Holy Spirit with God the Father and God the Son.

.... **8** The Holy Spirit's involvement in the lives of men began after Christ's resurrection.

.... **9** The baptism of Jesus provides an example of the perfect unity in the Trinity.

.... **10** The fact that the Holy Spirit imparts spiritual life is an evidence of His deity.

.... **11** The Holy Spirit is limited to one place at a time.

.... **12** The Holy Spirit's name reveals one of His divine attributes.

13 SELECTION. Draw a circle around the letter preceding each term which can be applied to the Holy Spirit.

a) Eternal
b) Incarnate
c) Sovereign
d) Limited
e) Unchanging
f) Holy
g) Omnipotent
h) Omnipresent
i) Omniscient
j) Angelic
k) Giver of life

SHORT ANSWER. Answer each question as briefly as possible.

14 In what way do the baptismal formula and the apostolic benediction give evidence of the deity of the Holy Spirit?

....

....

15 How can you benefit from the knowledge that the Holy Spirit is a divine Person?

....

....

answers to study questions

9 Your answer. Any of these:

a Romans 1:4.
b Hebrews 9:14.
c John 3:8; 1 Corinthians 2:4; Acts 10:38.
d Psalm 139:7-8; John 16:7-13; John 14:16-17.
e 1 Corinthians 2:9-11.
f Luke 1:35; Acts 1:8; Zechariah 4:6.

1 a John the Baptist told the crowd: "I baptize with water" but he said that Jesus would baptize them "with the Holy Ghost and with fire." Secondly, verse 22 reports that the Holy Spirit descended upon Jesus in the form of a dove.

b Luke 3:22: The voice of the Father came from heaven, saying, "You are my Son, whom I love; with you I am well pleased."

10 a the Holy Spirit.
b God.

2 He is seen ready for action at the outset of Creation. Verse 26 indicates a plurality in the Godhead. The implication is that the Holy Spirit was actively involved in Creation.

11 Second Peter 1:20-21 reveals that these statements were inspired of God and were not the result of human understanding. This Scripture *also* indicates a parity between God and the Holy Spirit in the initiation of and enablement for prophecy. The deity of the Holy Spirit is thus inferred.

3 Jesus was conceived in Mary by the power of the Holy Spirit.

12 a True
b False
c True
d True
e False

4 As Isaiah prophesied, the Holy Spirit came upon Jesus in anointing power that He might fulfill the ministry which the Father sent Him to do.

13 Your answer. I would reply: It is by the divine power of the Spirit of God that I can have eternal life and be freed from the bondage of sin.

5 b) a member of the Triune Godhead, coequal to the Father and Son, and in perfect unity with them.

14 The key is found in verse 13: Through the Spirit we must put to death the misdeeds of the body. Then we will live spiritually.

6 a 3) Genesis 2:18; Isaiah 1:14; 55:8. (Remember the elements of personality given in Lesson 1?)
b 5) Psalm 90:1-2.
c 4) John 14:23-26.
d 1) John 4:24.
e 6) Psalm 33:11; 102:25-27; Malachi 3:6.
f 2) 1 Corinthians 8:6.

15 c) the Holy Spirit power is infinite.

7 a command (or directive), call (or divine commission).
b man's wisdom.

16 a life.
b righteousness.
c omnipotent.
d omnipresent.

8 a 3) Holy.
b 5) Eternal.
c 1) Sovereign.
d 2) Omniscient.
e 6) Omnipresent.
f 4) Omnipotent.

LESSON 3

A HELPING PERSON

My home city is an automobile manufacturing center, so when I graduated from high school, I went to work in a car factory. I was given the job of pushing car bodies from one assembly line to another. The job needed two men, but the foreman was trying to cut expenses, so he said I would have to work alone.

Some of the big sedans were almost impossible for one man to push, and at the end of the day I was ready to quit. I had decided that the next day would be my last, but the next morning the foreman came by with a big, strong man and said, "Meet your new helper." All of my problems were over.

When Jesus came to the end of His earthly ministry, His few faltering disciples faced the impossible task of carrying on without His help. All their hopes seemed to die with Him when He was crucified. They were discouraged and went back to fishing. After His resurrection Jesus appeared to the disciples again and repeated His promise to send them another Helper.

There was no disappointment when the day finally arrived that the Holy Spirit came to be their Helper! He was everything they needed to help them fulfill the commission of Christ.

We have already seen that the Holy Spirit is a complete and divine Person. In this lesson we will study ways that He helps us, through conviction, regeneration, teaching, and counseling. Do you need more of his help in any of these areas? Open your heart as you study, and let the Holy Spirit be your personal Helper.

lesson outline

He Convinces
He Regenerates
He Teaches
He Counsels

lesson objectives

When you finish this lesson you should be able to:

- Explain what is meant by the *convincing* work of the Holy Spirit, based on John 16:7-11.
- Discuss the work of the Holy Spirit in *regeneration.*
- Describe the different aspects of the Holy Spirit's *teaching* and *counseling* ministry.
- Avail yourself of the *helping* ministry of the Holy Spirit.

learning activities

1. Study the lesson in the manner described in the learning activity for Lesson 1. Read the lemon content, find and read all Scripture texts given, and answer the study questions.
2. Find definitions in the glossary at the back of the study guide for any key words you do not know.
3. Take the self-test and check your answers.
4. Review Lessons 1-3, then answer the questions in Unit Student Report 1.

key words

anoints	intercessor	repentant
canon	interpreter	revelation
conviction	mediator	righteousness
enlightens	Paraclete	seal
inheritance	redemption	spokesman
inspire	regeneration	utterance

lesson development

HE CONVINCES

Objective 1. *Recognize true statements related to the ministry of the Holy Spirit in convincing the world of sin, righteousness, and judgment.*

The first work of the Holy Spirit in a person's life was explained by Jesus when He told the disciples He was sending a Helper to them. Here are His words:

> It is for your good that I am going away. Unless I go away, the Counselor will not come to you; but if I go, I will send him to you. When he comes, he will convict the world of guilt in regard to sin and righteousness and judgment: in regard to sin, because men do not believe in

me; in regard to righteousness, because I am going to the Father, where you can see me no longer; and in regard to judgment, because the prince of this world now stands condemned (John 16:7-11).

The world has set up its own list of standards of *sin* and *righteousness,* and it would like very much to ignore God's warning of *judgment.* Only because of God's great love for humanity has He sent the Holy Spirit to convince sinners that they are wrong. The Holy Spirit works in the unbeliever's heart to cause him to turn to the Lord, but He uses believers to testify to unbelievers about Jesus and live a holy life before them. Thus we might say that it is through the *believer* that He will prove the world wrong about sin and righteousness and judgment. He is our Helper in bringing the world to Christ.

Of Sin

When I gave an altar call in one of our evangelistic services, a beautiful little eight year old girl responded. She knelt at the altar with tears streaming down her cheeks and cried out, "Oh God, I'm such an awful sinner!"

I doubt that she had committed any of the sins that the world might label "awful," but the Holy Spirit had shown her the beauty of Jesus, and she was expressing her need of salvation. The world seldom considers the real sin of unbelief in God and disregard for the supreme gift of His Son, and yet it is the greatest of all sins. It was the Holy Spirit who revealed to the little girl her sinful state. Only the Holy Spirit can bring a person face-to-face with his condition and his rejection of Christ as Savior. Only the Holy Spirit can convince an unbeliever of his need to come to Christ in repentance and find forgiveness for his sin. Many times the Holy Spirit convicts sinners as they listen to the anointed preaching of the gospel (Acts 2: 14-41). On other occasions, conviction comes as a sinner hears the Spirit-anointed testimony of a believer who has accepted Christ as his Savior.

1 The Holy Spirit convicts the world of sin by
a) giving the unbeliever guidance in spiritual matters.
b) setting forth Jesus as the example of the life that pleases God (that He requires).
c) making sinners aware of their unworthiness to receive God's mercy.

Of Righteousness

Jesus said the Holy Spirit would convict (or convince) the world of righteousness because He was going to the Father.

Jesus' return to the Father was proof that everything He had said about Himself was true. If He had not been righteous, He would have died for His own sins, not ours. He would have remained in the grave and decayed like other sinful people. But He *was* righteous, He did pay the price for our sins, He arose from the dead, and He returned to the Father! That is why Peter set forth these truths so forcefully to his contemporaries on the Day of Pentecost (Acts 2:14-41).

The apostle Paul tells us in Romans 1:4 that Jesus "through the Spirit of holiness was declared with power to be the Son of God by his resurrection from the dead." It is the Spirit of holiness who bears witness of the righteousness of Jesus Christ. He brings glory to Christ by making the things of Christ known to the world (John 16:14).

2 According to the Acts record, which two answers are proof of the righteousness of Jesus Christ?
a) His teaching
b) His death on the cross
c) His resurrection from the dead
d) His return to the Father
e) His ministry among men

Of Judgment

The judgment that the Holy Spirit would use as an example to convince men of the certainty of judgment would be the judgment of Satan. His complete defeat at the hands of Jesus, and Christ's victory over hell and the grave, should be all that is needed to prove that there will be a final judgment.

Unless the preaching of judgment carries with it the love and concern of the Holy Spirit and emphasizes the victory of Christ, it will only turn men away from God. Jesus grieved when He warned Jerusalem of that was coming, and He showed no satisfaction whatever that those who would reject Him would be punished (Matthew 23:37-38).

We find many examples in the book of Acts of how the Holy Spirit used the apostles to convince people of sin, righteousness, and judgment. Peter spoke in prophetic utterance on the Day of Pentecost (Horton, 1976, p. 127). Here's what happened:

1. There was conviction of sin because of what their unbelief did to Jesus (Acts 2:22-23).
2. There was conviction of righteousness as the people recognized that God did not allow His Holy One to decay, but raised Him up to sit at His right hand (Acts 2:27, 30-33, 36).
3. There was conviction of judgment "With many other words he *warned* them; and he pleaded with them, 'Save yourselves from this corrupt generation'" (Acts 2:40).

4. The result was that the people at first began to despair. Then they repented and accepted Peter's message About 3000 were added to the number of believers that day.

Other examples are found in Acts 3:14-21; 4:10-12; 10:39-42; and 13:27-41.

The Holy Spirit is still our Helper today to bring the message of salvation to the world. He will use us to convince men of sin, of righteousness, and of judgment.

3 Circle the letter preceding TRUE Statements which describe the ministry of the Holy Spirit in convincing the world of sin, righteousness, and judgment, based upon the foregoing discussion.

a The sin that will bring eternal judgment is the sin of unbelief.
b The judgment that the Holy Spirit convinces us of is the judgment of sinful men.
c Christ's resurrection is a proof of His righteousness.
d The Holy Spirit's ministry to the world is mainly carried out by believers who witness by their lives and testimonies.
e Jesus' emphasis on judgment was that it was what sinners deserve.

HE REGENERATES

Objective 2. *Name three things the Holy Spirit does for us at the moment of our salvation.*

In a later lesson we will more fully discuss the Holy Spirit's work of *regeneration.* It is mentioned in this lesson to show the progression of the Spirit's ministry as our helping Friend from that of conviction of sin, righteousness, and judgment to that of constant Companion, Teacher, and Guide. Before we can experience the help of the Comforter in our daily lives, we must experience regeneration.

By *regeneration* we mean "rebirth." This is what happens when we turn from our sins and receive Jesus Christ as our Lord

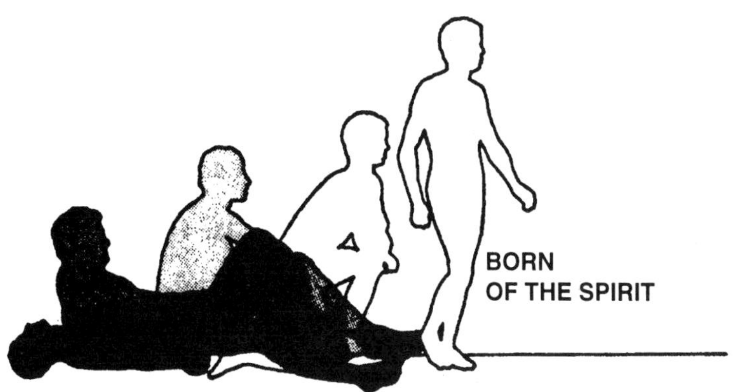

and Savior. It is the Holy Spirit who acts on behalf of the Father and the Son to impart spiritual life to the repentant sinner (John 3:3-8; 6:63; Titus 3:4-5).

At the moment of regeneration, the Holy Spirit *indwells* us; that is, He dwells within us and is ever present to help us (John 14:16-17).

4 Read Romans 8:9, 11; 1 Corinthians 3:16; 6:19 and explain the truth of these Scriptures by completing this sentence:

The moment we receive Christ as our Savior, the Holy Spirit

....

Having brought us to spiritual life, the Holy Spirit sets up residence in each believer. As He indwells us, He is God's seal or pledge—the down payment or deposit, which guarantees our future spiritual inheritance:

> And you also were included in Christ when you heard the word of truth, the gospel of your salvation. Having believed, you were marked in him with a seal, the promised Holy Spirit, who is a deposit guaranteeing our inheritance until the redemption of those who are God's possessions—to the praise of his glory (Ephesians 1:13-14).

5 On the basis of John 14:1-3, Ephesians 1:12-13, and 2 Corinthians 1:22, the Holy Spirit is called our *deposit* because

....

....

The seal of the Holy Spirit represents the security that we have in Him as He controls our lives. It also testifies to our sonship, which means that we will share in the inheritance of our heavenly Father (Romans 8:15-17; Galatians 4:6).

Thus, the Holy Spirit initiates spiritual life in us in the new birth experience. As He indwells us, He is in a position to control the course of our lives. His presence brings confidence to us He makes our sonship meaningful by 1) testifying to its reality (Romans 8:16), 2) inspiring hope in us as we look to the future benefits which sonship guarantees for us, 3) praying and interceding for us so that we pray according to the will of God (Romans 8:26-27), and 4) reminding us that His activity in our lives is a pledge or seal of God's presence that brings daily assistance to help us maintain an acceptable spiritual life.

6 Name the three things we have discussed in this section which the Holy Spirit does for us at the moment of regeneration.

....

HE TEACHES

Objective 3. *Identify what Jesus meant when He said the Holy Spirit would teach us "all things."*

Communicating truth to believers is one of the important ways the Holy Spirit is a helping Person. This is why Jesus called Him the *Spirit of truth* in the same sentence in which He called Him the Counselor or Comforter (John 14:16-17). Teaching and counseling are closely linked in the ministry of the Holy Spirit. We will discuss three aspects of the Holy Spirit's teaching ministry. Remember that this ministry is to the *believer.*

Instructor

Just as Jesus came to make known the nature and will of the Father, so the Holy Spirit comes to make known the nature and will of Jesus (John 14:20-21, 23-26). One way He did this in times past was to inspire Jesus' followers to record the Master's life and ministry. This is the record of the Gospels: Matthew, Mark, Luke, and John.

How would the Holy Spirit teach? *First, He would glorify Christ.* He would not teach an entirely new and unrelated body of knowledge; rather He would take the things that Christ taught, shed additional light on them, and enable the hearers to grasp the desired truth. As believers grow and develop in spiritual maturity, they are able to shoulder more responsibility. They change from a milk diet to that of solid food (1 Corinthians 3:2 and Hebrews 5:11-14). While the spiritual diet changes, the subject, Jesus Christ, remains the same.

The Comforter leaves out nothing that is important for you to know about Jesus Christ. "He will teach you all things" Jesus promised (John 14:26). You may wonder, "Doesn't He care about my job, my family, my financial status?" Yes, God does care! Jesus, however, taught us to recognize our priorities: "But seek first his [the Father's] kingdom and his righteousness, and all these things [your material, physical, social, and vocational needs] will be given to you as well" (Matthew 6:33). The Holy Spirit teaches us how to order our lives appropriately in the spiritual realm, and then with Him in control of our lives, He leads us appropriately in other areas of life. It is the Holy Spirit who reveals to us the deeper things of God and helps us to understand spiritual things (1 Corinthians 2:10-15). In all of this, His purpose is to glorify Christ. Stanley M. Horton says, "The Holy Spirit always reveals Jesus as all the Bible says He is" (1976, p. 121).

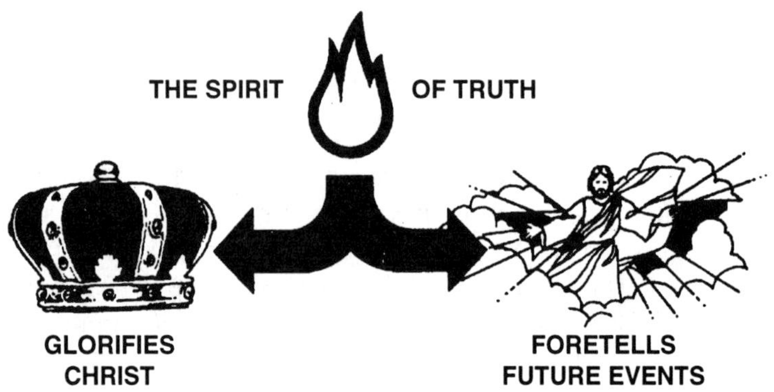

Second, a knowledge of future events was included in the things the Holy Spirit would teach. "He will tell you what is yet to come," Jesus said (John 16:13). This promise became much clearer when the apostle John was *in the Spirit* on the Lord's day and was given the revelation of Jesus Christ (Revelation 1:10). John was told that these were things which *must soon take place.* The revelation included a record of events which would occur from the first century after Christ until the time of the New Heaven and the New Earth (Revelation 21). Under the same inspiration Paul spoke of the Lord's appearing (1 Thessalonians 4:13-18), the conditions surrounding His appearing (1 Thessalonians 5:1-11), God's judgment on unbelievers (2 Thessalonians 1:5-12), and the appearance of the man of lawlessness (2 Thessalonians 2:1-12). Peter also spoke under the Spirit's anointing about the coming Day of the Lord (2 Peter 3:1-13). The common element we see in all these events is the coming revelation of the glory of Jesus Christ.

7 What is the theme that runs throughout the book of Revelation?
a) The judgment of sinners
b) The glory of Jesus Christ
c) Satan's final victories

8 Based upon the foregoing discussion, when Jesus said that the Holy Spirit would teach us "all things," what did He mean? Circle the letter preceding the answers you choose.

a) All that God wants us to know about Himself
b) All that we need to know about our occupation
c) Specific events about our future life on earth
d) All that God wants us to know about Jesus
e) Things of the Spirit that will help us to glorify Christ
f) Future events that relate to our spiritual life in Christ
g) How to be financially successful
h) How to convince the world of sin, righteousness, and judgment

Objective 4. *Describe the function of the Holy Spirit in relation to the writing of Scripture.*

As the Gospels were written, the Holy Spirit began His ministry of interpreting them. The apostle Paul was the one chosen to explain the gospel in detail to the church. His Epistles to the church make up the greatest part of the New Testament Scriptures following the four gospels and the book of Acts. Other apostles and New Testament believers were also inspired by the Holy Spirit to *take the things of Christ and make them known* (John 16:14). How did this occur?

Second Peter 1:20-21 and 2 Timothy 3:16 reveal the mechanics of biblical revelation. These Scripture references disclose the fact that the Holy Spirit inspired men to record God's Word as it was given to them. The human writers did not initiate the process; rather, they spoke and wrote faithfully God's message as they were enabled by the Holy Spirit. The serious student of the Word of God will notice that while the message is God's, it is recorded in the individual style and with the unique vocabulary of each writer, and in some cases, the writer's background experience is clearly evident. The writers were not simply mechanical robots; they were sensitive to God's Spirit and recorded precisely the message God intended, lending their own faculties to this process.

Although the canon of Scripture has been closed, and all that God intended to reveal has already been recorded in the Bible, the Holy Spirit continues His ministry of interpretation. He takes the things that have been written and *illuminates* them (makes them clear) to the hearts and minds of believers.

The best way to understand any book is to ask the author what he meant when he wrote it. The problem is, not many authors are available to us, but the Holy Spirit is! All the human writers of the Bible died centuries ago. What comfort it is to know that the divine Author is with us forever! Every time you open your Bible, your personal Helper is by your side to help you understand it.

9 According to the Scripture references we have consulted in this section, which of the following is the best description of the function of the Holy Spirit in the writing of Scripture?

a) The Holy Spirit caused men to write what He revealed in the same style, vocabulary, and literary form so that each part of the Bible would be the same as every other part.
b) As the Holy Spirit moved upon holy men of God, they fell into trances. Being unconscious, they simply recorded what was dictated. In this case, the Spirit did not employ the writers' style, vocabulary, or a given literary form.
c) The Holy Spirit prompted chosen men of God to prophesy. As the Spirit moved them, they faithfully recorded God's message. In the process of communicating God's message, the Spirit employed each writer's vocabulary, style, and background experience.

Spokesman

Objective 5. *Relate the word* spokesman *to the ministry of Jesus, the Holy Spirit, and the believer.*

The Comforter would be God's spokesman after Jesus returned to His Father in heaven. A spokesman is one who speaks as the representative of another. Jesus had been a perfect witness and speaker for God, but He had finished the work the Father had given Him to do. Jesus told His disciples that when the Spirit of truth came, He would speak (John 16:13).

Jesus, as the Father's spokesman, had said, "My teaching is not my own. It comes from Him who sent me" (John 7:16). The same would be true of the Comforter: "He will speak only what he hears" (John 16:13).

The difference would be that Jesus spoke through His own physical body, while the Comforter would speak through believers. When we speak for Him, it is usually a message the Holy Spirit has given us as we have studied God's Word. He enlightens and anoints us as we study, and we become spokesmen for God. In this way, God can have spokesmen all over the earth at the same time, because our Helper is omnipresent. He can speak through each of us as we listen to Him and allow Him to speak through us.

There will be those times also, as we will study later, when the Holy Spirit speaks directly through us by the gifts of the Spirit. We actually do the speaking, but He is giving us the words to Speak at the time the gift is in operation. Any believer can speak for God, but only as he receives the message from the Holy Spirit (1 Corinthians 12:1-10).

10 Read John 14:7 and 26, and answer these questions:

a What spokesman revealed to us what God is like? ....

b What spokesman reveals to us what Jesus is like? ....

c When the Holy Spirit speaks through us, what will He remind us of?

....

d To be a spokesman means to ....

....

HE COUNSELS

Objective 6. *Match the different aspects of the Holy Spirit's counseling ministry with the definition of each.*

In Lesson 1 we learned that the Greek word *Paraclete* in John 14:16 is translated in different versions of the Bible as *Comforter, Helper,* or *Counselor.* This word literally means "one called alongside to help." In thinking of the Holy Spirit as our Counselor, the meaning seems to be that of a friend who appears as an intercessor, guide, or comforter. All of these aspects of the Holy Spirit's personal ministry to us fit in well with the idea of one called alongside to help. How can we apply these ministries to our personal lives?

Intercessor

In the same way, the Spirit helps us in our weakness. We do not know what we ought to pray, but the Spirit himself intercedes for us with groans that words cannot express. And he who searches our hearts knows the mind of the Spirit, because the Spirit intercedes for the saints in accordance with God's will (Romans 8:26-27).

The apostle Paul refers here to the Spirit as our Intercessor (one who prays or petitions in behalf of another). In our times of weakness, we don't know what to pray for and how to pray. In our times of weakness, we often fail to understand what we really need and how to seek appropriate solutions. We may want to please God and do His will above all else in our lives, but we don't know how to reconcile present difficulties with God's larger purpose of bringing us to spiritual maturity. At such times, the Spirit comes to our assistance and intercedes for us with groans that cannot be expressed in words. God the Father knows what is in our minds and what is in the mind of the Spirit. Since there is perfect communication between the Father and the Holy Spirit, there is no need for *words.* Because the Spirit knows the Father's thoughts and will, we can have confidence that He intercedes according to the will of God. This knowledge should help us believe that our prayers will be answered in God's way and in God's time.

I have experienced times in prayer when the burden was so great that I did not know how to express it to God. I have actually sensed the presence of the Spirit within me, making known to God my petition which I was unable to put into words. How precious it is to know that we have a helping Friend who takes up our petition when we don't know how to pray!

A missionary friend was very ill in Africa and was rushed to a hospital for surgery and the premature delivery of her son by cesarean section. At the very moment that her crucial time began, the father of a dear friend in America was awakened from sleep with a heavy burden to pray for Marie. He prayed through the night, and throughout the next day he continued to pray, refusing food or rest. On through the second night he prayed. The morning of the second day he rose from his knees and reported, "God has answered my prayer!" Later that day his daughter received a cablegram from the missionary friend in Africa which said, "Our son was born yesterday. Marie and baby doing fine." It was the Holy Spirit, our Intercessor, who impressed upon this godly man the need to pray and intercede for a friend thousands of miles away.

The Holy Spirit also helps our intercession by reminding us of the things that are ours in Christ and assuring us of the things God wants to do for us (1 Corinthians 2:12). Without His help our prayers would be an empty form.

11 In this section on the Intercessor we have seen that the Holy Spirit helps us to pray in what two ways?

....

....

12 Which of these illustrate the intercessory ministry of the Holy Spirit? Circle the letter preceding the answers you choose.
a) "I made a list of all my needs and presented them to God in prayer."
b) "I knew that my brother had a deep spiritual need, but I didn't know how to pray about it. All I could do was surrender to the Holy Spirit as He reached to God in my brother's behalf."
c) "My family had no food to eat. While we were praying, there came a knock at the door. A friend from our church stood there with a bag of groceries. God had already provided the answer before we prayed."
d) "Since God is more aware of my needs than I am, it really isn't necessary for me to spend much time in prayer."

Guide

What career shall I choose? Whom should I marry? Where should I live? You are faced with important decisions every day, and you need a reliable guide. Your success will depend on the kind of guidance you follow.

There are many voices offering advice, each claiming to be the best. There is only one Counselor who is completely safe to follow. He is the Counselor Jesus promised to send. When you must decide between truth and error, He will lead you in the path of truth, because He is the Spirit of truth. His guidance always leads to true success (1 John 4:1-6).

"Live by the Spirit"—that is, walk in the Spirit, be led by the Spirit (Galatians 5:16,18). "Since we live by the Spirit, let us keep in step with the Spirit"(Galatians 5:25). To keep in step with Him, we must be willing to let Him guide our steps. He will direct us as we live in accordance with Him and desire what He desires (Romans 8:5). As we acknowledge His sovereign leadership, He will guide us progressively into all truth (John 16:13). He will also direct us, as He did the early church members, into favor with other people. He will undoubtedly provide for us also as He did for them: economically, vocationally, and spiritually (Acts 2:42-47).

In addition to His function as our guide into truth and in the practical direction of our daily lives, the Holy Spirit also reveals the serious nature of our misdeeds—the behaviors associated with our old, unregenerate nature (compare Ephesians 4:20-32 with Romans 8:12-14), Moreover, besides revealing the pitfalls of the path that lies ahead of the one who tends to come under the control of the old self, the Spirit also helps him put to death any conduct that is inconsistent with the new self. Or, the Spirit may simply check us on occasion from following a course of action that is not consistent with God's will *at the time*. It was not sin for Paul and his company to desire to evangelize in Asia; it was just not God's time (Acts 16:6-10), Later, this *check* was removed and Paul had a tremendous ministry in this province (Acts 19:10). These functions of the Holy Spirit as our guide are important to us in our spiritual development.

13 Read the Scriptures (right), and match each to the kind of guidance it indicates (left). Place the number of your choice in each blank space.

. . . . **a** Decision-making	1) Acts 8:29
. . . . **b** Prevention	2) Acts 13:2
. . . . **e** Appointment	3) Acts 15:28
. . . . **d** Direction	4) Acts 16:6

We have seen that the Holy Spirit not only gives us what we *should* do (decision-making, appointment, and direction) but He also guides us in what we should *not* do, forbidding us to move ahead of Him or to act in ways that are inconsistent with our status as sons of God (compare Romans 8:12-16 with 1 John 3:2-3). We must look to Him for guidance and obey His voice.

Comforter

As we have said, the word *Paraclete* is sometimes translated as *Comforter.* The Holy Spirit is our Comforter in the sense of One "called alongside to help." The comfort of the Holy Spirit is not divine pity. He knows the sorrows of life and does have compassion but His comfort is much more than sympathy.

Among other characteristics with which He graces our lives, the Holy Spirit produces peace (Galatians 5:22). His peace is the product that results when our lives are surrendered to His control (Romans 8:6). As we become increasingly aware of His control over our lives, we become aware of our spiritual sonship—that we belong to God. This produces a feeling or sense of belonging which the Spirit reinforces. This knowledge should give us a tremendous sense of security and peace.

His comfort includes *hope.* No matter how dark the night, the Comforter, who knows the future perfectly, lets you know there will be a morning, and that the promise of Jesus, "I am coming back to you," will be fulfilled (John 14:28).

14 Match the different aspects of the Holy Spirit's counseling ministry (right) with the definition of each (left). Write the number representing your choice in each blank space.

.... **a**	The Spirit leads us through discipline, prevention, appointment, direction, decision-making..	1) Intercessor 2) Guide 3) Comforter
.... **b**	The Holy Spirit gives us peace and hope even in the most difficult circumstances.	
.... **c**	The Holy Spirit helps us when we pray by reminding us of needs, and by praying for us when we are unable to express our deepest needs.	

15 Have you experienced the Holy Spirit's help in any of these areas? If so, write the words *Intercessor, Guide*, and *Comforter* in your notebook, and beside each describe the personal experience you have had of the ministry of your helping Friend. Thank Him for being with you and ministering to all of your spiritual and daily needs.

You have now concluded Unit 1, *A Personal Friend.* You have been taught that the Holy Spirit is a *complete* Person, a *divine* Person, and a *helping* Person. He wants to dwell within you to teach you and counsel you.

In the next unit of study you will discover that the Holy Spirit is also a *powerful* Friend. God bless you as you continue your study!

self-test

MULTIPLE CHOICE. Select the one best answer to each question. Circle the letter preceding the answer you choose.

1 Which of these is NOT a translation of the Greek word *Paraclete?*
a) Comforter
b) Counselor
c) Creator
d) Helper

2 Which of these is a literal definition of *Paraclete?*
a) One who convinces
b) One called upon to judge
c) One who sympathizes
d) One called alongside to help

3 Which of these is NOT a part of the Holy Spirit's *convincing* ministry. He convicts the world of all of these except
a) judgment.
b) regeneration.
c) righteousness.
d) sin.

4 The word *regeneration* in relation to the Holy Spirit's ministry describes
a) spiritual birth.
b) physical birth.
c) the death and resurrection of Christ.
d) trying to live a better life.

5 The judgment which the Holy Spirit convinces the world of is the judgment of
a) believers.
b) unbelievers.
c) Satan.

6 Which of these, according to our study, is NOT a work of the Holy Spirit at the moment of our salvation?
a) He disciplines us.
b) He seals us.
c) He regenerates us.
d) He indwells us.

7 Which word is NOT associated with the work of the Holy Spirit when He puts His seal upon us?
a) Ownership
b) Security
c) Guarantee
d) Perfection

8 The Holy Spirit reminds us of needs we should pray about, and He presents our needs to God with groans that cannot be expressed in words. This is His ministry as our
a) Teacher
b) Comforter
c) Intercessor
d) Interpreter

9 Decision-making, prevention, appointment, and direction are related most closely to the Holy Spirit's function as our
a) Guide
b) Comforter
c) Mediator
d) Convincer

SHORT ANSWER. Answer each question as briefly as possible.

10 Name two things that Jesus said the Holy Spirit would do in His teaching ministry to us.

....

....

11 List in the proper order the spokesmen who have passed on the revelation of God to mankind.

From God ...., ...,

.... to the world.

> Before you continue your study with Lesson 4, be sure to complete your unit student report for Unit 1 and return the answer sheet to your ICI instructor.

answers to study questions

8 I would circle a), d), e), f), and h). Answers b), c), and g) are not specific things that the Holy spirit teaches us, although He does give us wisdom to apply ourselves to practical matters as well as spiritual.

1 b) setting forth Jesus as the example of the life that pleases God (that He requires).

9 c) The Holy Spirit prompted chosen men of God.

2 c) His resurrection from the dead.
d) His return to the Father.

10 a Jesus.
b The Holy Spirit.
c Everything that Jesus taught.
d speak in behalf of someone else.

3 a True.
b False.
c True.
d True.
e False

11 Sometimes He brings needs to our minds so that we can pray about them. At other times He presents them directly to God when we cannot find words to express them.

4 (In your own words.) Dwells within us; comes to live in us.

12 Answers b) and c) illustrate the intercessory ministry of the Holy Spirit.

5 He is the seal or guarantee that Jesus will return for His own, as He promised in John 14. The Holy Spirit is our guarantee or deposit of a future inheritance.

13 a 3) Acts 15:28.
b 4) Acts 16:6.
c 2) Acts 13:2
d 1) Acts 8:29.

6 He regenerates us, He indwells us, and He seals us.

14 a 2) Guide.
b 3) Comforter.
c 1) Intercessor.

7 b) The glory of Jesus Christ.

15 Your answer.

UNIT TWO

THE HOLY SPIRIT: A POWERFUL FRIEND

LESSON 4

THE SPIRIT IN CREATION

A Christian astronomer was traveling cross-country by train, on his way to deliver a lecture. In his baggage was one of the first battery-powered scale models of the solar system, which he had constructed and was using in his lectures. An atheist sat down beside him on the train. In the course of their conversation, the atheist began to ridicule the idea of a divine creation of the universe.

The astronomer listened quietly for a while. Then he invited the atheist to accompany him to the baggage car. There he removed the cover from his model and pressed the switch. As the little planets orbited the sun in perfect harmony, the atheist was much impressed "Magnificent," he said "Who designed this?" The astronomer smile "No one designed it," he replied. "It all came together by an accident of nature."

The atheist was silent. These were the very words he had used to explain his ideas about the beginning of the solar system after which the astronomer had patterned his model. If the model needed a creator, how much more did the original design!

The earth, the heavens, and all that dwells in them are the handiwork of a divine Creator. It was by the power of the Holy Spirit that the spoken word of God was put into effect. In this lesson we will study the work of the Holy Spirit in Creation. Our divine, personal Friend was there when the world was formed, and He is still active in our lives today in creative power.

lesson outline

Cooperating in Creation
Creating the World
Creating Man
Sustaining All Things

lesson objectives

When you finish this lesson you should be able to:

- Discuss what the Bible reveals about the involvement of the Father, Son, and Holy Spirit in Creation.
- Explain ways in which the creation of man differed from the rest of Creation.
- Recognize examples of the power of the Holy Spirit in Creation and in sustaining His creation.

learning activities

1. Study the lesson in the manner described in the learning activities for Lesson 1. Read the lesson content, find and read all Scripture texts given, and answer the study questions.
2. As background for this lesson, read Genesis, chapters 1 and 2 and John chapter 1.
3. Find definitions in the glossary at the back of the study guide for any key words you do not know.
4. Take the self test and check your answers.

key words

astronomer	hover	sustaining
astronomy	impartation	universe
celestial	preexistence	vegetation
finite	solar system	

lesson development

COOPERATING IN CREATION

The Pre-Creation Planners

Objective 1. *Explain why the Genesis account of Creation is not more specific about the involvement of the Son and the Holy Spirit in the Creation.*

"In the beginning God . . ." (Genesis 1:1). These opening words of the Bible in the Hebrew language use a *plural* name of God. Although the Son and the Holy Spirit are not specifically named, the Triune God is implied.

The doctrine of the Trinity is part of God's progressive revelation of Himself that was not developed until the writing of the New Testament. At the time that Moses wrote the Pentateuch (first five books of the Old Testament) many people were polytheistic (believed there were many gods). A revelation of the Triune God at that point in time would have brought confusion. God knew that the people were not ready to receive this truth, so He did not reveal it. His self-revelation is progressive because He knows exactly how much to reveal at any given time. Thus, the Creation account in the book of Genesis does not give us all of the details of God's creative work. Other Scriptures help us to understand the role of each person of the Trinity in God's creation plan as well as in His redemptive plan.

The book of Genesis talks about many beginnings: of creation, of man, of sin, of judgment, and of redemption. Only the first two chapters tell about Creation. The Creation account is recorded briefly as a background to the early events in man's history leading to his need for redemption.

Even *before* Creation God already knew what would happen to His creation. He anticipated that man would sin, and He made a provision for man's salvation. Several Scriptures reveal this to us:

1. Revelation 13:8 speaks of the book of life belonging to the Lamb (Jesus) that was slain from the foundation (creation) of the world.

2. Ephesians 1:4 tells us that God chose us in Christ before the creation of the world.

3. Matthew 25:34 refers to a kingdom prepared for the faithful since the foundation of the world.

Several Scripture references confirm the eternal existence of the Triune God. Thus, we know that the Father, Son, and Holy Spirit, who always act in perfect unity, planned and carried out the creation of all things together. Let's look at some of these Scriptures:

1. In Psalm 90:2 the psalmist declares: "Before the mountains were born or you brought forth the earth and the

world, from everlasting to everlasting you are God." *This is a reference to the preexistence of the Father.*

2. The apostle John declares *the preexistence of the Son* in John 1:1: "In the beginning was the Word, and the Word was with God, and the Word was God. He was with God in the beginning." John goes on to say, "The Word became flesh and lived for a while among us. We have seen his glory, the glory of the one and only Son, who came from the Father, full of grace and truth" (John 1:14). The Son was there at Creation in equal presence with the Father.

3. The presence of the Holy Spirit at Creation is implied in Hebrews 9:14, where He is called the *eternal Spirit.* He is without beginning or ending, and He was present with the Father and the Son at Creation. The *preexistence of the Holy Spirit* is confirmed by this reference to His eternal nature.

The Father, the Son, and the Holy Spirit were present in the beginning. The Triune God, who caused everything else that exists, is Himself the "uncaused cause"—that is, He has always existed, and He will always exist. Our finite minds cannot fully grasp this truth, because we are time oriented. God is timeless. Before the *beginning* spoken of in Genesis 1:1, the Father, Son, and Holy Spirit in perfect unity decreed the plan of Creation as well as the plan of Redemption.

1 Based on the text, give a reason for the Genesis account of Creation not being more specific about the involvement of the Trinity.

....

....

2 Read the first chapter of Genesis and answer these questions:

a How many times is God mentioned in this chapter? ....

the Holy Spirit? .... the Son? ....

b We believe that verse 1 implies the Trinity because a plural name is used for God. What other verse implies the Trinity?

....

The Co-Creators

Objective 2. *Describe ways that the Father, Son, and Holy Spirit were involved in Creation.*

Scripture also very clearly assigns the act of Creation to all of the members of the Trinity.

1. When the early church members prayed to God, they said, "Sovereign Lord you made the heaven and the earth and the sea, and everything in them" (Acts 4:24). They were obviously praying to the Father.

2. Again, in the beginning of John's Gospel he spoke these words concerning the Son: "Through him all things were made; without him nothing was made that has been made" (John 1:3). Clearly Jesus was involved in creation.

3. In a beautiful psalm of praise, Creation is described as a work of the Holy Spirit. In Psalm 104:30 the psalmist declares, "When you send your Spirit, they are created, and you renew the face of the earth." This speaks not only of the Spirit's involvement in creating the earth, but also in sustaining it.

Creation is the result of perfect cooperation of the Father, the Son, and the Holy Spirit. We don't fully understand how this took place. Stanley Horton says, "The Father is the Creator, the Maker. He created through the Son and by the Spirit. The mystery of how this was done is not explained in the Bible in any detail. The attention is on the fact that He is the Creator and we are His creatures" (Horton, The *Holy Spirit,* p. 52).

We will see that the Holy Spirit took an active part in all of creation. He is specifically mentioned as *moving* in creative power, which is a dominant feature of many of His activities (See Job 33:4; Psalm 104:30; John 6:63; and also Romans 8:11 for reference to the Spirit's life-giving power.)

3 Even though the creation account in Genesis does not emphasize the involvement of all of the three persons in the Trinity, how do we know that the Father, Son, and Holy Spirit were equally involved?

....

....

CREATING THE WORLD

Objective 3. *Distinguish between true and false statements regarding the events of Creation.*

Bible scholars, among others, have given many theories to explain the darkness and void that covered the earth before the acts of creation began. Since the Word of God does not reveal the reason to us, and we can only suppose what may have brought it about, we will not attempt to discuss it here. We know from Scripture that it was a condition of emptiness and ruin which only the operation of the Spirit of God could transform into the fullness and beauty that followed.

Moving on the Waters

> Now the earth was formless and empty, darkness was over the surface of the deep, and the Spirit of God was hovering over the waters (Genesis 1:2).

The foregoing verse pictures the Holy Spirit hovering over the pre-creation universe. Deuteronomy 32:11 uses the same verb to describe a mother bird hovering or fluttering over her young in an energetic, protective way. The dynamic spiritual energy of the third Person of the Trinity is revealed here as ready to carry out the creative decrees of God. The series of creative commands that followed were His to carry out. He is revealed as the active agent of Creation.

The first command came: "Let there be light" (Genesis 1:3). Immediately there was light, and it was good.

The second command came: "Let there be an expanse between the waters to separate water from water" (Genesis 1:6). The foggy mist lifted and became clouds above the waters by the action of the Holy Spirit. One interpretation of Job 26:13 describes what happened: "By His breath [Spirit] the skies became fair."

The third command was given: "Let the water under the sky be gathered to one place, and let dry ground appear" (Genesis 1:9). The oceans surged back as the omnipotent energy of the Spirit of God operated within and upon it. Whole continents emerged from the waters and became dry land.

4 Which of these words best describes the involvement of the Holy Spirit in separating the waters?

a) Restful
b) Waiting
c) Commanding
d) Powerful

Moving in the Earth

The commands that follow (Genesis 1:11-13, 20-25) regarding the earth portray the Holy Spirit as the Spirit of Life. We saw earlier that this is one of the titles given to Him.

He moves over the vast lands of the earth's continents, and they begin to produce all kinds of vegetation suited to the condition of their climate (Genesis 1:12). He moves in the oceans and lakes and rivers, and they are filled with unnumbered creatures. Beautiful birds fill the air (vs. 20-22). He moves again over the land and gives the breath of life to every kind of animal (vs. 24-25).

The singer of Psalm 104 praises God especially for this part of Creation, and says, "When you send your Spirit, they are created" (Psalm 104:30). It is obvious from the context that *they* refers to the living creatures that populate the waters and lands of our earth (see Psalm 104:24-25).

The variety and beauty of plants, animals, fish, and fowl leave us in awe as to the capacity of their Creator. In the African museum in Brussels, Belgium, there is an enormous variety of plant and animal life from the continent of Africa. One of the most interesting displays is of hundreds of delicate, intricate, and colorful insects and bugs. Some of them have the appearance of tiny jewels sparkling in the sunlight. This is just a minute part of the great variety in God's creation. It was the Holy Spirit who put God's plan into action in creative power.

5 Read Genesis 1:11-12 and 20-25. These Scriptures reveal that God created

a) every kind of vegetation, sea creatures, birds, and animals.
b) certain kinds of vegetation, sea creatures, birds, and animals from which a larger variety developed.
c) a small number of each type of living thing which produced other types.

Moving in the Heavens

> By the word of the Lord were the heavens made, their starry hosts by the breath of his mouth (Psalm 33:6).

In this Scripture the Psalmist records the creation of the heavens by the Spirit (breath) of God. The Genesis account of creation focuses on the earth and the placement of heavenly bodies as its lights (Genesis 1:14-18).

No study reveals the awesome power of God as much as a study in astronomy (the science of the celestial bodies, such as stars). Our universe has such enormous dimensions, to comprehend it goes beyond the ability of our imagination. As human beings we are but specks of dust on the earth, and the earth seems less than a speck of dust in proportion to the universe.

Distances in the universe are so great, our earthly means of measurement seem totally inadequate. For example, measurements in deep space must be based on the speed of light, which travels 186,000 miles (299,270 kilometers) per second. Distances in space are not measured by seconds or minutes, or even hours or days. The measurements are in *light years*!

The nearest star outside our solar system is four and one-half light years away. In other words, its light takes four and one-half years to reach us traveling at 186,000 miles a second. At the present time, astronomers can observe stars three billion light years away from the earth!

To give you some idea of the *number* of stars that were made by the breath (Spirit) of God, there are 100 billion stars in our galaxy (a galaxy is one of many systems of stars). Astronomers have observed more than a billion galaxies of stars.

Jeremiah spoke for humanity when he used the expression "as countless as the stars of the sky and as measureless as the sand on the seashore" (Jeremiah 33:22). The Psalmist David proclaimed the wonder of God's creation in Psalm 19:1: "The heavens declare the glory of God; the skies proclaim the work of his hands." What a mighty God we serve! This same Holy Spirit who carried out the Father's decrees as the agent of Creation is working in our lives today; His power is available to us to carry out the Father's will in the world that He formed so amazingly.

6 Circle the letter in front of TRUE statements concerning the events of creation.

a Each Person of the Godhead was responsible for a different part of the Creation.

b The Spirit's hovering over the pre-Creation waters gives the idea that His dynamic energy is ready to carry out the creative decrees of God.

c Even though the universe is enormous beyond our power to imagine, every part of it works in perfect harmony with other parts.

d God created the earth, its vegetation, animals, birds, and sea creatures out of nothing.

e The Genesis account of Creation focuses on the heavens and how they were formed.

f The sun, moon, and stars arc celestial bodies created by God.

g One of the things the Spirit did at Creation was to give the breath of life to living creatures.

CREATING MAN

Objective 4. *State what gave man life and how this differed from the creation of other beings.*

Designed by God

"Then God said, 'Let us make man in our image, in our likeness'" (Genesis 1:26). Again there is the plural name of God, followed by plural pronouns. The Godhead is seen planning a special manifestation of divine love.

We described man as a speck of dust when he is compared to the size of the universe. To God he is a very special "speck of dust." He is the crowning work of God's creation and the peculiar object of His divine love.

Revelation 13:8 reveals that man's salvation was planned before creation. This divine decision (Genesis 1:26) must have taken place before the beginning of time. Let's try to imagine what took place in the Godhead. "Let us design a being like ourselves," the Father said, "a being that can think and feel and make decisions—a spiritual being we can communicate with—a being with whom we can have close communion."

In making this plan, God determined to give man full freedom to accept or reject the love of his Creator. In His omniscience, He knew that man would fall into sin, and that it would be necessary to provide a way for him to renew his fellowship with God. The Son of God would be called upon to make the supreme sacrifice. He willingly offered Himself. The Holy Spirit would be the one to carry out the plan. God knew that there would be a select company who would by an act of will choose to follow Him. This company of believers would be partakers of His own nature. Even before the act of Creation God worked out the plan of salvation.

> So God created man in his own image, in the image of God he created him; male and female he created them (Genesis 1:27).

7 Why did God work out the plan of salvation even before He created man?

....

....

Formed by God

"And the Lord God formed man from the dust of the ground" (Genesis 2:7). Other species of life came into existence as God spoke the word and the Holy Spirit moved over the face of the earth.

Man was different. God personally molded his body from the dust of the ground. His creation was distinct from all other creative acts. Chapter 2 of Genesis gives us fuller details about some of the creation events in chapter 1. In Genesis 2:21-22 we see that the creation of man was made complete when God took one of the man's ribs and made a woman from the rib he had taken out of the man.

Quickened by God

And the Lord God . . . breathed into his nostrils the breath of life, and man became a living being (Genesis 2:7). The Spirit of God has made me; the breath of the Almighty gives me life (Job 33:4).

To *quicken* means to give life. First God formed the body. Then the Spirit of God breathed into it, bringing to life the spiritual person who would inhabit the body. The living being which came from the breath of God seems to be more of an *impartation* of the Holy Spirit than a creation. Some element of creation is there, but the living being comes from the breath of the Almighty.

While we are considering here both facts and powers beyond our human ability to understand, it is safe to say that the creation of man gives him a place of closeness with God that none of God's other creatures possesses.

8 At what point in the creation of man did he receive life?

....

9 In what way was the creation of man different from the rest of creation? ....

....

10 This difference points out that, of all God's creatures, man is a
a) physical being.
b) spiritual being.
c) being of no greater importance in God's sight than any other.

SUSTAINING ALL THINGS

Objective 5. *Identify Scriptures which reveal activities of the Father, Son, and Holy Spirit in sustaining creation.*

Just as all three Persons of the Trinity were involved in the creation of all things, so are they active in sustaining creation. Many Scriptures speak of God preserving His people (see Deuteronomy 6:24; Psalm 31:23; Proverbs 2:8; 2 Timothy 4:18). Psalm 121 declares:

> I lift up my eyes to the hills—where does my help come from? My help comes from the Lord, the Maker of heaven and earth. He will not let your foot slip—he who watches over you will not slumber; indeed, he who watches over Israel will neither slumber nor sleep.
>
> The Lord watches over you—the Lord is your shade at your right hand; the sun will not harm you by day, nor the moon by night.
>
> The Lord will keep you from all harm—he will watch over your life; the Lord will watch over your coming and going both now and forevermore.

Jesus, you will recall, said He would ask the Father to send the Counselor to be our constant Companion (John 14:16). It is He who watches over us day and night, and we are safe in His care. His watchful care extends not only to us but also to the entire created order.

11 Read Job 12:7-10. What is it that the animals, the birds, and the earth, and the fish of the sea teach us?

....

12 Read Isaiah 40:7 and 13. State in your own words what these verses mean to you. ....

....

13 Read each Scripture listed (right), and match each with the activity it describes (left).

.... **a** Jesus sustains all things by His Word.	1) Psalm 104:30
.... **b** We need not fear, because God will strengthen and uphold us.	2) Hebrews 1:1-3
.... **c** The Spirit who created all things also renews all things.	3) Isaiah 41:10

14 These Scriptures reveal that both creation and the preservation (care) of all that was created is
a) mostly the work of the Holy Spirit.
b) mainly an activity of God the Father.
c) carried out by the Father, Son, and Holy Spirit.

As we behold the magnitude of God's creation, we must stand in awe and amazement at the wonders He has performed. Surely He is worthy of our honor and praise. When He completed His work on the sixth day and observed all that He had done, He said that it was very good.

God created all things for His glory. "The heavens declare the glory of God; the skies proclaim the work of his hands" (Psalm 19:1). His creation reveals His glory. He created us that we might glorify Him. Many Scriptures exhort us to glorify God (see 1 Chronicles 16:29; Psalm 29:1; Romans 15:6, 9). Do you glorify God your Creator? Do you honor Jesus, the Son, and the Holy Spirit who has come to dwell within you?

There is no better conclusion to this lesson than the words of the four and twenty elders who fell down before the Creator and cast their crowns before His throne (Revelation 4:11, KJV):

Thou art worthy, 0 Lord, to receive glory and honor and power: for thou has created all things and for thy pleasure they are and were created.

self-test

MULTIPLE CHOICE. Circle the letter in front of the best answer to each question.

1 Which of these completions is correct concerning the amount of revelation the Genesis account gives to the participation in Creation of the Godhead? The Genesis account reveals
a) that all three Persons of the Trinity were fully involved, and details are clearly given.
b) little about individual involvement, but it emphasizes the plurality of the one eternal God and that He is the Creator of all things.
c) that the Holy Spirit had the greatest involvement in Creation.

2 Which of these is given the most emphasis in Genesis?
a) Creation of the universe
b) Beginning of sin and judgment
c) Man's need for redemption
d) Creation of man

3 God's plan of salvation was decided
a) before the beginning of time.
b) alter man sinned.
c) at the time Jesus was born.
d) at the time of Creation.

4 Psalm 90:2, John 1:1, and Hebrews 9:14 confirm the eternal nature of God by reference to
a) the presence and involvement of the Triune God at Creation.
b) the preexistence of the Trinity in relation to the time of Creation.
c) the preexistence of the Father, with the Son and Holy Spirit appearing later in time.
d) the condition of darkness and void at the time of Creation.

5 Creation is an operation of
a) the Father, the Son, and the Holy Spirit.
b) the Father and the Holy Spirit.
c) God and man.

6 The Spirit's activity in the Creation of the world was to
a) speak the Word.
b) decide what was to be done.
c) move in power to carry out the divine decree.

7 What was the Holy Spirit's involvement in the creation of man?
a) Forming man from the dust of the earth.
b) Making woman from the rib of the man.
c) Imparting the breath of life which made man a spiritual being.
d) Hovering over man in creative power.

8 Following creation, the Holy Spirit's involvement with the created order may be described most accurately as
a) sustaining all that was created.
b) showing concern for people who obeyed God.
c) gradually populating the earth with new forms of life.

9 God created man and the world because He wanted to
a) be complete.
b) display His glory and receive glory.
c) have control of something.

10 In what way can we best glorify God for all that He has done?
a) Enjoy the beauties of nature
b) Worship and obey Him
c) Show kindness to all His creatures
d) Take as much control as possible of all living things

11 In what way was the creation of man different from the rest of Creation?
a) Man is the only creature who came into being as an adult.
b) Man was formed by God from dust, and then God breathed into him the breath of life; the rest of Creation was by the spoken word.
c) Man was given the power to sustain all other things.

12 Why was God's revelation of Himself progressive rather than complete at the time Moses wrote the Pentateuch?

a) Because His divine nature was not fully developed at that time.
b) The people were not ready to receive the revelation of a Triune God.
c) Moses did not understand the revelation of the Trinity clearly enough to explain it so that it would be understood.

answers to study questions

8 When God breathed into his nostrils the breath (Spirit) of life.

1 The people were not ready for the full revelation of the Trinity at that time—it would have confused them.

9 All other created things were spoken into existence by God as His Spirit moved over the earth. God formed man from dust and gave him life with His own breath.

2 a At least 30; once; not at all.
b Verse 26 (plural pronouns *us* and *our*).

10 b) spiritual being.

3 Other Scriptures throughout the Bible clearly give credit to the Godhead (the Trinity) for Creation.

11 The life and breath are in the hand of the Lord.

4 d) Powerful.

12 Your answer. I believe they indicate that the Spirit of God has given us life, and He has control over the beginning and ending of our lives.

5 a) every kind of vegetation, sea creatures, birds, and animals.

13 a 2) Hebrews 1:1-3.
b 3) Isaiah 41:10.
c 1) Psalm 104:30.

6 a False.
b True.
c True.
d True.
e False.
f True.
g True.

14 c) carried out by the Father, Son, and Holy Spirit.

7 He knew that man would not keep his fellowship with Him and that a provision would have to be made to restore that fellowship.

LESSON 5

THE SPIRIT WHO COMMUNICATES

Since Creation, God has communicated with His people by various means. In the Old Testament He spoke through the Holy Spirit to the prophets, who passed on God's message to the people. Some prophets and other men chosen by God recorded His message so it could be passed from one generation to the next.

Jesus was the Living Word of God, anointed of the Holy Spirit, He came to show us what God was like. The Gospels record His teaching and the details of His ministry on earth. The written record came from men who walked and talked with Him, and they wrote through the inspiration of the Holy Spirit.

After Jesus ascended into heaven, the apostles continued to communicate God's message. Several of them were inspired by the Holy Spirit to write the message, giving us the canon of Holy Scriptures. In all of this communication, God has worked through the Holy Spirit to give His Word to men and women so that they will know and obey Him.

In this lesson we will see the work of the Holy Spirit in bringing us the written Word, in anointing the Living Word, and in making us living Epistles. Today the Holy Spirit communicates God's message through you and me, and we are responsible to pass it on to others.

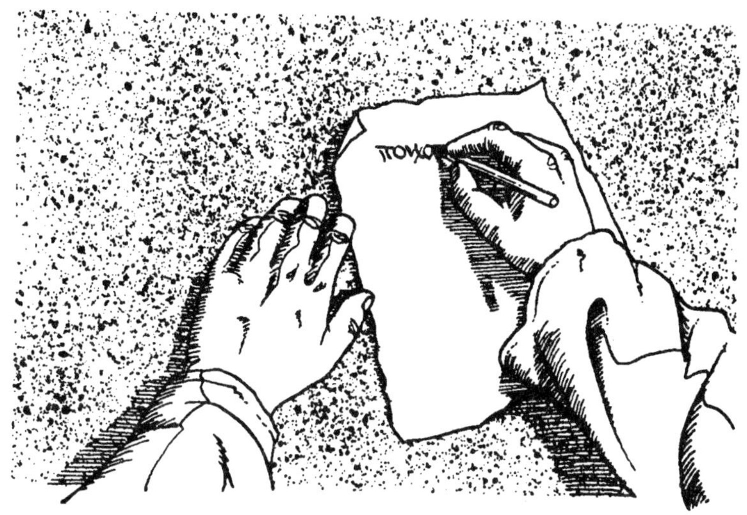

lesson outline

The Written Word
The Living Word
Living Epistles

lesson objectives

When you finish this lesson you should be able to:

- Define the terms *revelation, inspiration* and *illumination* as they apply to the work of the Holy Spirit.
- Explain ways we can know the Bible is the Spirit-inspired Word of God.
- Describe the role of the Holy Spirit in the life and ministry of Jesus.
- Demonstrate an understanding of the importance of being a living Epistle by allowing the Holy Spirit to work through you.

learning activities

1. Study the lesson in the manner described in the learning activities for Lesson 1. Read the lesson content, find and read all Scripture texts given, and answer the study questions.
2. Find definitions in the glossary at the back of the study guide for any key words you do not know.
3. Take the self-test and check your answers.

key words

anointing
descent
illumination
infallible
inspiration
ordeal
unblemished

lesson development

THE WRITTEN WORD

A Writing Needed

Objective 1. *Differentiate between examples of revelation, and inspiration and illumination.*

God's message to man is a life-and-death matter. The Psalmist David said, "I have hidden your word in my heart that I might not sin against you" (Psalm 119:11).

God's desire to communicate His message to men and women is made very clear by the writers of the Old Testament. The words "Thus said the Lord" or similar words are used more than 3800 times. It is by hearing the Word of God and acting upon what we hear that we are saved from eternal death.

The first time God gave the Ten Commandments to Moses, He wrote them Himself:

> Moses . . . went down the mountain with the two tablets of the Testimony in his hands. They were inscribed on both sides, front and back. The tablets were the work of God; the writing was the writing of God, engraved on the tablets (Exodus 32:15-16).

Moses broke those tablets when he saw the sin of the people. A second time God gave the Ten Commandments to Moses with these instructions: "Write down these words, for in accordance with these words I have made a covenant with you and with Israel" (Exodus 34:27). Verse 28 reports that "Moses wrote on the tablets the words of the covenant—the Ten Commandments."

Why is a written communication better than an oral one? Because an oral message passed from person to person usually changes each time it is passed on.

A game called *gossip* is an illustration of this. The players sit in a circle. A message is written on a piece of paper and held by the first person. Then it is whispered from ear to ear all the way around the circle. By the time the last person repeats it to the first, the message can hardly be recognized as the one that was written.

If the written message itself had been passed around the circle, each player would have received it in its purest form. The last person would have received the same message as the first.

God's message to man must be received exactly as God delivered it. No one has permission to change it even a little. This is why it was necessary for the Holy Spirit to give us the complete, *infallible* Word of God in written form. *Infallible* means "without error." God's message had to be written so that it would not change as it was spoken from person to person. It had to be complete so that no one would need to add to it or subtract from it to his own liking, and it must be infallible. While it does not treat every aspect of our present and future existence exhaustively, God has revealed what He wanted us to know about salvation, maintaining spiritual life, our responsibility to Him and our fellow man, and the future of sinner and saint. The Bible may be regarded as our all-sufficient rule for faith and practice. It is the full revelation that God intended to communicate to us, and it is entirely trustworthy. Because of these things we can trust it without doubt or reserve.

When God wishes to communicate with His people, He does it through the agency of the Holy Spirit. There are three ways the Holy Spirit communicates to people: by *revelation,* by *inspiration,* and by *illumination.*

1. *Revelation* is the revealing, or making known, of something previously not known. When the Holy Spirit speaks to someone directly and tells him something he has no other way of knowing, it is a *revelation.*

2. *Inspiration* is the moving of the Holy Spirit upon a man's intellect or emotions to express the mind of God. When the Holy Spirit used the Bible writers, to record the truth without making mistakes, that was *inspiration.* This truth could be things they already knew, or it could be by revelation of the Holy Spirit (2 Timothy 3:16).

Christian leaders and scholars often refer to the *plenary inspiration* of Scripture. *Plenary* carries the idea of fullness. Therefore, *plenary inspiration* means that Scripture, in its fullest extent, was inspired by the Holy Spirit.

The *verbal inspiration* of Scripture is often referred to, also. Scripture teaches us that spiritual truth is expressed in spiritual words (1 Corinthians 2:13). *Verbal inspiration* means that not just the ideas but the very words of Scripture are inspired by the Holy Spirit.

3. *Illumination* is the clarifying of something, the shining of a light upon something. *Illumination* occurs when the Holy Spirit helps either the writers or the readers to understand what is being written.

All of these forms of communication are used by the Holy Spirit in giving us God's message and making it come alive in our hearts. God's written Word, the Bible, was given to us by the inspiration of the Holy Spirit, because a written record was needed.

1 Read Isaiah 9:6-7. In this Scripture Isaiah foretold the birth of Jesus. This is an example of
a) illumination.
b) revelation.
c) inspiration.

2 If while you are reading in Matthew 8 about the healing of the man with leprosy and the many other healings of Jesus, you realize that Jesus is also able to heal you, the Holy Spirit has given you
a) revelation.
b) verbal inspiration.
c) illumination.

3 Fill in the blanks with the correct words.

a Second Timothy 3:16 supports the .... inspiration of Scripture; that is, Scripture in its fullest extent was inspired by the Holy Spirit.
b First Corinthians 2:13 supports what we call .... inspiration of Scripture; that is, the very words were inspired by the Holy Spirit.

c When we say that God's Word is ...., we mean that there are no errors in it.

4 State in your own words why a written record of God's revelation to man was needed.

....

....

A Writing Protected

Objective 2. *Explain the factor that has caused God's written Word to be kept free from error with the passage of time.*

Paul told Timothy, "All Scripture is God-breathed . . ." (2 Timothy 3:16). This simply means that the writing of all Scripture was controlled by the Holy Spirit. Paul's words are further explained by the apostle Peter (2 Peter 1: 20-21):

> Above all, you must understand that no prophecy of Scripture came about by the prophet's own interpretation. For prophecy never had its origin in the will of man, but men spoke from God as they were carried along by the Holy Spirit.

In other words, the prophets and apostles who wrote the Bible were watched over and inspired by the Holy Spirit so that the words they wrote are what God wanted them to write—they are without error and can be called the Holy Scriptures.

About 40 writers contributed to the miracle book we call the Bible. They came from many different places and lived over a period of about 16 centuries. While their writings differ in expression and style, there is a supernatural unity in their message, because the guiding intelligence behind them was the Holy Spirit.

The Bible's unity is remarkable in view of the number of men God chose to write it and the period of time over which they wrote it. One Bible scholar points out that there is *one* doctrinal viewpoint, *one* moral standard, *one* plan of salvation, *one* program of the ages, and *one* world view in the Bible (Thiessen, 1979, p. 67). This was possible only because of the inspiration of the Holy Spirit upon those who did the writing.

The divine authorship of the Bible is confirmed by the writers of the Scriptures themselves. In 2 Samuel 23:2, in his last song to Israel, David said, "'The Spirit of the Lord spoke through me; his word was on my tongue.'" Jesus confirmed the fact of David's inspiration as recorded in Samuel by stating, "David himself speaking by the Holy Spirit, declared...." (Mark 12:36) Again, in Hebrews 3:7 the writer quotes Psalm 95, introducing it with these words: "So, as the Holy Spirit says ...." These examples demonstrate that the writers of Scripture acknowledged the divine authorship of the Scriptures. Jesus' testimony also reinforces this fact.

God's written Word has also been carefully protected as it has been copied over and over again and passed down from one generation to the next. This again is the work of the Holy Spirit. Certainly He would not carefully watch over the original writings of the Scriptures and then allow them to become unreliable documents when they were copied and handed down to us.

Here again, we believe the Holy Spirit has carefully guarded His divine communication so that our present Bible can be safely called the Word of God. Many people have tried to prove the Bible to be wrong or to assert that it contains errors, but their efforts are in vain. God's Word is as reliable today as it was when it was first written!

5 In your own words explain the factor that has caused God's written Word to be kept free from error with the passage of time.

....

....

PROTECTED BY THE SPIRIT

A Writing Recognized

Objective 3. *Give scriptural proofs that the Bible is recognized as the work of the Holy Spirit and is still proving its divine authorship today.*

The Old Testament as we have it was accepted as valid by Christ and the apostles, who referred to Old Testament Scriptures often in their teaching. They also recognized it as the work of the Holy Spirit.

6 Match each New Testament Scripture (right) with its related Old Testament Scripture (left). Place the number representing your choice in each blank space.

. . . . **a** Matthew 22:43-44	1) Proverbs 25:21-22
. . . . **b** Luke 4:18-19	2) Jeremiah 31:33
. . . . **c** Acts 2:17-21	3) Isaiah 61:1-2
. . . . **d** Romans 12:20	4) Psalm 110:1
. . . . **e** Galatians 3:11	5) Habakkuk 2:4
. . . . **f** Hebrews 10:15-16	6) Joel 2:28-32

The influence of the Holy Spirit can also be observed in the gathering of the New Testament writings and their recognition and acceptance by the early church leaders.

By the fourth century A.D. the church had developed eastern and western divisions, which were influenced by the Greek and Latin cultures. The Holy Spirit's influence is seen as each division of the church accepted as Scripture the same 27 books that are now the New Testament. Each division of the church came to its decision independently, and both decisions came within a period of just thirty years.

Over the 16 centuries that have followed, this Book of books has been recopied thousands of times and translated into almost every known language. Wherever it is preached, believers recognize it as the Word of God, and lives are changed as the Holy Spirit makes its truths understood to the people of all nations.

In 1778 the French writer, Voltaire, predicted that in 100 years the Bible would no longer be in circulation, but that his own works would be widely published. Today the Bible is still the best-selling Book in the world, translated into more languages than any other book, and its message is preached everywhere. Voltaire's works, in comparison, are known and read by a very limited number of people.

Wherever God's Word is preached, the Holy Spirit is active to illuminate the Word and make it come alive in the hearts of men and women, bringing them to repentance and acceptance of Jesus Christ as their personal Savior. We recognize the Bible as God's Word, inspired by the Holy Spirit, because it changes the lives of those who hear it and receive it, just as the Scriptures say it will do.

7 Find these Scriptures in your Bible, and complete the chart by writing the Scripture text beside the statement of what Scripture says about itself.

Deuteronomy 8:3	1 Peter 2:2	Mark 16:15-20
John 15:3	John 17:17	1 John 5:13
Isaiah 40:8	1 Peter 1:25	Psalm 119:103
1 Peter 1:22	Psalm 126:6	Mark 4:14-20
Psalm 119:89	Matthew 5:18	1 Kings 8:56
Romans 15:4	Psalm 119:9	Ephesians 5:25-26

GOD'S SPIRIT-INSPIRED WORD TELLS US THAT IT:	
a will endure	
b is food for our soul	
c cleanses us	
d gives us hope	
e bears fruit	
f is trustworthy	

THE LIVING WORD

Preparing the Word

Objective 4. *Describe ways the Holy Spirit was involved in the preparation of Jesus for His earthly ministry.*

"The Word became flesh..." (John 1:14) is one of the most meaningful statements in the Bible. It describes God the Son becoming a human being so that deity could communicate with humanity on humanity's level. Before the Word became flesh, God had spoken at many times and in various ways through the prophets, but now He would communicate directly with man through His Son.

Just as the Holy Spirit was the agent of God at Creation, so He was active in moving upon the virgin Mary in creative power. Luke tells us of the visit of the angel Gabriel to Mary, foretelling *the birth of Jesus.* The angel told her:

> "The Holy Spirit will come upon you, and the power of the Most High will overshadow you. So the holy one to be been will be called the Son of God" (Luke 1 :35).

Later, Luke tells us that Mary went to visit her relative Elizabeth, and when she greeted Elizabeth, "Elizabeth was filled with the Holy Spirit. In a loud voice she exclaimed: 'Blessed are you among women, and blessed is the child you will bear!'" (Luke 1:41-42).

Matthew's Gospel sheds further light on the role of the Holy Spirit in the incarnation: "She [Mary] was found to be with child through the Holy Spirit" (Matthew 1:18). Thus, He who was "in the very nature God" took "the very nature of a servant, being made in human likeness" (Philippians 2:6-7). Very God and very man—Jesus became flesh through a unique act of the Holy Spirit and lived for a while among us (John 1:14). Later we read Jesus' words concerning this preparation: "'Sacrifice and offering you did not desire, but a body you prepared for me'" (Hebrews 10:5).

The Holy Spirit continued to be active in the preparation of Jesus for His earthly ministry. While we do not read of the Spirit's active involvement in Jesus' human development, the implication from what we have learned is that what the Spirit initiated in bringing about the birth of Jesus, he sustained. Luke says, "And Jesus grew in wisdom and stature, and in favor with God and man" (Luke 2:52).

John the Baptist reveals the unique presence of the Holy Spirit in Jesus' life on the occasion of His baptism: "'I saw the Spirit come down from heaven as a dove and remain on him'" (John 1:32). John testified further that God had given him the sign that on whomever he saw the Spirit descend and remain, the same was the Son of God (vs. 33-34). The presence of the Spirit in Jesus' life seems to indicate that He was there to anoint Jesus for ministry, as we shall see.

The descent of the dove (the Holy Spirit) upon Jesus was a visible manifestation which everyone could see. It was immediately followed by the voice of God from heaven saying, "'You are my Son, whom I love; with you I am well pleased'" (Luke 3:22).

Stanley Horton points out that "the dove to the Jews was more than a symbol of gentleness and peace. It was also the sin offering which the poor substituted for the lamb (Leviticus 5:7). Jesus is God's own Lamb provided as a substitute for the poor, the needy, the sinful of this world, which includes us all (Romans 3:23)" (Horton, 1976, p. 90).

Chapter 4 of Luke emphasizes the presence of the Holy Spirit in preparing Jesus for His earthly ministry.

8 What does verse 1 tell us about the activity of the Holy Spirit?

....

....

Jesus was tempted by the devil for 40 days. It is clear that the *temptation of Jesus* occurred while He was being led by the Spirit. Every phase in the training and development of Jesus was under the watchful care of the Holy Spirit! Chapter 4 also tells us that after the devil finished his tempting (and failed in his effort) Jesus returned to Galilee *in the power of the Spirit.*

9 List the three instances mentioned in the text which prepared Jesus for His ministry when the Holy Spirit was present and actively involved.

....

Anointing the Word

Objective 5. *Give examples of ways the Holy Spirit anointed the ministry of Jesus.*

Shortly after He returned to Galilee, Jesus went to His home town of Nazareth and visited the synagogue. On this occasion the scroll of the prophet Isaiah was handed to Him. He chose the 61st chapter of Isaiah and read these prophetic words describing His own ministry:

> "The Spirit of the Lord is on me, because he has anointed me to preach good news to the poor. He has sent me to proclaim freedom for the prisoners and recovery of sight for the blind, to release the oppressed, to proclaim the year of the Lord's favor" (Luke 4:18-19).

10 What did Jesus say as soon as He finished reading this Scripture? (v. 21)

....

His *ministry* confirmed His claim to the anointing of the Holy Spirit. He cast out demons by the Spirit of God (Matthew 12:28). According to the apostle Peter, Jesus' healing and deliverance ministry resulted from the anointing of the Holy Spirit on His life (Acts 10:38). Everything that Jesus said He would do under the anointing of the Spirit, He did in His earthly ministry!

You may find it interesting and helpful to read the four Gospels and to make a list of the healings of Jesus, the blind eyes opened, the multitudes who were fed miraculously, the deaf who were healed, the dead who were brought back to life, and the demon possessed who were delivered and given freedom from the devil's bondage. All these are manifestations of the Holy Spirit's work in Jesus' ministry.

11 Glance through chapters 8 and 9 of Luke and list the activities of Jesus described in these two chapters. Can you see that they are a fulfillment of Isaiah's prophecy?

....

....

In Matthew 12:34 Jesus said, "For out of the overflow of the heart the mouth speaks." What is in your heart will come out in your words. Would you like to know what is in the heart of God? The Holy Spirit presents Jesus as the Word of God. Study His words and deeds. He is a perfect expression of the heart of God.

Crowning the Word

Objective 6. *Recognize in what way the Holy Spirit crowned the ministry of Jesus and made it possible for man to be fully restored to fellowship with God.*

The message of God's love involved more than preaching, teaching, healing the sick, or casting out devils. It meant also the death of God's Lamb for the sins of the world.

The cross was a horrible ordeal, but Jesus endured it willingly, with the help of the Holy Spirit. He who knew no sin had to take upon Himself the sins of the world and give His life as the perfect sacrifice for sin. The writer to the Hebrews tells us how He was able to do it: ". . . Christ, who through the eternal Spirit offered himself unblemished to God" (Hebrews 9:14). In speaking of Christ's death and resurrection, Peter testified to the Jews, "We are witnesses of these things, and so is the Holy Spirit . . . " (Acts 5:32).

The Spirit was present in creative power when Jesus became flesh; He was present in anointing power throughout Christ's ministry; He was present in strengthening power in Christ's ministry; He was present in strengthening power in Christ's great hour of need on the cross; and He was present in resurrection power to give victory over death. He is the Spirit that raised up Jesus from the dead (Romans 8:11).

Just before He ascended to His Father, Jesus showed that those who believed in Him were fully restored to fellowship with God. He breathed on His disciples and said, "'Receive the Holy Spirit'" (John 20:22).

In the beginning the breath of God had made man a living soul. Now, in a token meeting of believers just before He returned to the Father, God the Son breathed on man again, symbolizing that by the power of the Holy Spirit spiritual life is fully restored to those who will believe on Jesus and obey His Word. This would appear to be the crowning act of Jesus' ministry. Because of the resurrection, which indicated Christ's victory over sin and death, man could be reconciled to God. Spiritual death could now be overcome by believing on the Lord Jesus Christ.

12 What made it possible for Jesus to endure the cross and give His life for us?

....

13 In which of these ways did the Holy Spirit crown the ministry of Jesus and make it possible for man to be fully restored to fellowship with God? Through His

a) creative power.
b) anointing power.
c) strengthening power.
d) resurrection power.

THE LIVING EPISTLES

Objective 7. *Find examples in given Scriptures of responsibilities we have to be living epistles, taught, empowered and ruled by the Holy Spirit.*

Taught by the Spirit

Jesus knew well the weaknesses and the strengths of His disciples. Many times He rebuked them for their unbelief and wrong attitudes, but always His plan was that after He was gone they would preach His gospel. The whole future of His work on earth depended on them. They would make Him known. How could He entrust His disciples with such responsibility when He was no longer there to guide them?

The answer is simple. It centered in the divine Person who was coming to take His place as their Helper. The same Spirit that rested upon Him would come upon them. After Jesus had finished His work and was glorified, the disciples would receive the Holy Spirit, and He would instruct them and give them power to become faithful witnesses.

In His role as Counselor, Jesus said the Holy Spirit would teach His followers. The Counselor would bless them with the ability to recall the Master's teachings. We can be sure that the Counselor not only reminded them of Jesus' spoken words but also of His matchless example in responding to the many and varied needs of people (John 14:26; 15:26). Moreover, in the course of their learning, Jesus said that the Counselor would guide them into all truth. This implies the fact that the Spirit of truth would give them the ability to discriminate between His truth and the spirit of falsehood (compare John 16:13 with 1 John 4:1-6). He would also give them insights into the future with a well-balanced knowledge of the relationship between present responsibilities and future reward.

The teaching which Christ's followers received and which they were to pass on to others was not written on tablets of stone such as Moses received on Mount Sinai. It was not simply "head knowledge" that had little relation to practical living, nor was it written, as Paul's letters were, with pen and ink. The teaching they had received was "internalized," that is, it had become a part of them, for it was written on the fleshly tablets of their hearts by the Holy Spirit, as Paul wrote to the Corinthians:

> You show that you are a letter from Christ, the result of our ministry, written not with ink but with the Spirit of the living God, not on tablets of stone but on tablets of human hearts (2 Corinthians 3:3).

The message becomes a part of the messenger when it is inscribed on his heart by the Holy Spirit. He truly becomes a *living letter.*

LIVING LETTERS

TAUGHT, EMPOWERED, RULED BY THE SPIRIT

Are you a living letter? Has God's message been written on your heart by the Holy Spirit? Are you faithful to pass His message on to others?

14 Match the Scripture references (right) with the appropriate description of the Holy Spirit's teaching function that is either stated specifically or implied (left).

.... **a** The man who is taught by the Spirit develops spiritual discernment.	1) Corinthians 2:13
.... **b** What the believer speaks is on a spiritual level, since he is taught by the Spirit to express spiritual truth in appropriate spiritual terms.	2) Acts 1:8
.... **c** The Holy Spirit's function is to teach and to remind one of all that is Christ's.	3) John 14:26
.... **d** The ability to know the vast storehouse of spiritual knowledge and experience which is one's spiritual inheritance, comes from the Holy Spirit.	4) Corinthians 2:12
.... **e** The Spirit teaches us about our weaknesses and wrong acts, and He helps us to overcome.	5) Corinthians 2:14
.... **f** The Spirit enlightens us concerning our responsibility to share our experience.	6) Romans 8:13

Empowered by the Spirit

To be an effective *living* epistle, one must have the power of the indwelling Spirit. Jesus knew this when He admonished, "Let your light shine before men, that they may see your good deeds and praise your Father in heaven" (Matthew 5:16). He also knew the importance of the Spirit's enablement when He gave the challenge to His followers to preach repentance to all nations. Thus, He challenged them to "stay in the city until you have been clothed with power from on high" (Luke 24:49), the gift of the Holy Spirit with which they were to be baptized (Acts 1:4-5). Paul recognized the relationship between exemplary Christian living and the empowering of the Spirit. Thus, in Romans 8 he instructs Roman believers to allow the powerful Helper to control their lives (v. 6) and to triumph over behavior that is unbecoming to a believer (v. 13). With the Spirit's help we have confidence of our sonship and future inheritance (vs. 15-17). This knowledge enables us to face the dilemmas of life with serenity and peace, because fear has been replaced by security (v.15). We can be unperturbed in the storms of life because of the Counselor's help; we can thus reflect His peace and love as living epistles should.

15 Read 1 Peter 3:8-16. What effect will being a living epistle have on those who speak evil of your Christian behavior, according to the apostle Peter?

....

....

Ruled by the Spirit

As a living epistle, Paul said, you are "known and read by everybody" (2 Corinthians 3:2). It is important that the same Holy Spirit who wrote the message on your heart controls the motives and attitudes of your life. You must communicate God to the world. You can be sure that the world will be watching your behavior as well as listening to your message. Your actions will, indeed, speak louder than your words.

Galatians 5:13-26 very clearly shows us what our life in the Spirit should be like. When we are led by the Spirit, we cannot do as we please. The freedom we have in Christ is not to be used to indulge in sinful pleasure, but it is to be a means of expressing the love of Christ to a sinful world.

This Scripture gives us two lists that are in sharp contrast to one another. One list describes the acts of the sinful nature. The other describes the acts of one who is ruled by the Spirit. The acts of the sinful nature are selfish acts which have no concern for others; the actions of one who is ruled by the Spirit are expressions of love toward others The only way we can communicate God's message to other people effectively is under the control and guidance of the Holy Spirit.

16 Complete the following chart by listing the acts of the sinful nature and the attitudes of one who is ruled by the Spirit.

GALATIANS 5:19-23	
Column A Acts of the Sinful Nature	**Column B** Attitudes When Ruled by the Spirit

17 Read Romans 8:1-8 and answer these questions.

a Describe our state of being when we are ruled by our sinful nature.

....

b How does this condition change when we are ruled by the Spirit?

....

To conclude this lesson, read Luke 4:18-19 again. In this Scripture, Jesus, the living Word, proclaimed what He came to do under the anointing of the Holy Spirit. He demonstrated His obedience by His life and actions. John reminds us that if we truly love God and acknowledge the Lordship of Jesus, our faith will enable us to overcome the world. This refers to our "being" before God. Our behavior under the control of the Spirit will be acceptable to God. John also says that if we love God we will obey His commands. We will demonstrate our love in practical ways. May each of us aspire to "be" what God wants us to be and "do" the things He wants us to do. Then we will bring glory to his Name

self-test

MULTIPLE CHOICE. On the basis of our discussion, select the one best answer for each question. Circle the letter preceding your choice.

1 We are saved from eternal death by hearing the Word of God and

a) telling others what we heard.
b) remembering what we heard.
c) acting upon what we heard.

2 God wanted His Word written because He knew that an oral message

a) could reach more people.
b) changed as it was passed on.
c) would always be the same.
d) was more reliable.

3 When we say that God's written Word is infallible we mean that it is

a) inspired in part by the Holy Spirit.
b) written by godly men.
c) composed by many books written over a long period of time.
d) without error.

4 The making known of something previously not known is called

a) inspiration.
b) revelation.
c) illumination.
d) communication.

5 If we believe in plenary inspiration this means that we believe

a) Scripture in its fullest extent was inspired by the Holy Spirit.
b) the men who wrote the Scriptures did not really understand what they were writing.
c) the Holy Spirit gave God's message to men who wrote it according to their own understanding.
d) most Scriptures were inspired by the Holy Spirit.

6 It is by the illumination of the Holy Spirit that believers are able to
a) understand which Scriptures are inspired.
b) explain their feelings to God.
c) understand the meaning of Scriptures.

7 In view of the number of men who wrote the Bible and the period of time over which it was written, which of these is the most remarkable?
a) The Bible's unity
b) The similarity in writing style throughout
c) The changing customs it describes
d) The influence of the Holy Spirit in all of the writing

8 The factor that kept God's written Word free from error even with the passage of time was
a) the control of the church.
b) the confirmation of Jesus that it was the Word of God.
c) the guidance of the Holy Spirit.

9 One important proof that the Bible is the work of the Holy Spirit is that it
a) has been translated into many languages.
b) is recognized as God's Word even by nonbelievers.
c) is still doing today what it says it will do in the lives of men.

10 The first visible manifestation of the Holy Spirit upon Jesus was at
a) His birth.
b) His baptism.
c) His temptation.
d) His resurrection.

11 Jesus' claim to the anointing of the Holy Spirit is confirmed by
a) His ministry.
b) His death.
c) His resurrection.
d) all of these answers
e) answers a) and c).

12 The only way we can be living epistles is to be
a) ruled by the Spirit.
b) ruled by our own spirit.
c) preachers or evangelists.

answers to study questions

9 In His birth, in His baptism, and in His temptation.

1 b) revelation. (If you said *inspiration* you are also correct. The facts concerning the future were given by revelation; whereas, by means of inspiration the prophet was enabled to record accurately the message he received from God.)

10 "Today this Scripture is fulfilled in your hearing."

2 c) illumination.

11 Women cured of evil spirits; parables and teaching; calming the storm; healing of a demon-possessed man; healing of a sick woman; raising of a girl from the dead; sending out of the twelve disciples to preach and heal the sick; feeding of the five thousand; the transfiguration; healing of a boy with an evil spirit.

3 **a** plenary
b verbal
c infallible

12 The strengthening power of the Holy Spirit.

4 Your answer. I would say it was needed because a written message is more trustworthy than a message passed by mouth (that is, it remains the same). Also, a written message makes *all* of God's Word available for everyone. It is complete and unchanging.

13 d) resurrection power.

5 The Holy Spirit who controlled the writing of the Scriptures has also protected them as they have been copied and passed down from one generation to the next.

14 a 5) 1 Corinthians 2:14.
b 1) 1 Corinthians 2:13.
c 3) John 14:26.
d 4) 1 Corinthians 2:12.
e 6) Romans 8:13.
f 2) Acts 1:8.

6 a 4) Psalm 110:1.
b 3) Isaiah 61:1-2.
c 6) Joel 2:28-32.
d 1) Proverbs 25:21-22.
e 5) Habakkuk 2:4.
f 2) Jeremiah 31:33.

15 Peter says that evil speakers will be ashamed of their slander. Such Christian behavior will demonstrate powerfully the claims of the gospel to transform lives.

7 a Psalm 119:89; Isaiah 40:8; Matthew 5:18; 1 Peter 1:25.
b Deuteronomy 8:3; Psalm 119:103; 1 Peter 2:2.
c Psalm 119:9; John 15:3; John 17:17; 1 Peter 1:22; Ephesians 5:23-26.
d Romans 15:4; 1 John 5:13.
e Psalm 126:6; Mark 4:14-20; Mark 16:15-20.
f 1 Kings 8:56 (also Matthew 5:18).

16 Column A:

Sexual immorality, impurity, debauchery, idolatry and witchcraft, hatred, discord, jealousy, fits of rage, selfish ambition, dissensions, factions and envy, drunkenness, orgies, and such things.

Column B:

Love, joy, peace, patience, kindness, goodness faithfulness, gentleness, and self-control.

8 Jesus was full of the Holy Spirit, and He was led by the Spirit into the desert.

17 a Our minds are set on pleasing our sinful nature.

b Our minds are set on pleasing God.

LESSON 6

THE SPIRIT WHO REGENERATES

Have you ever looked at a tiny baby and marveled at the miracle of birth? This tiny creation which began as two cells invisible to the naked eye now contains all that is necessary to grow and become a mature, intelligent, responsible adult. Even more amazing, those two tiny cells that joined together to make a new life contained all of the components which would emerge in the child as mother's red hair, father's bone structure, grandfather's disposition, grandmother's teeth, or Uncle Charlie's sense of humor! Yet the child will become an individual with his own distinct characteristics, unlike any other that ever lived, and responsible to God for his own choices.

Provision has been made not only for our physical development but also for our spiritual rebirth. This provision is possible through the activity of the Holy Spirit in our lives, convicting of sin, bringing repentance, coming to dwell within us, and adopting us into the family of God. It is as we cooperate with the Holy Spirit that we are given new life in Christ, and we become joint heirs with Him in the inheritance that our heavenly Father has prepared for us. Spiritual birth brings with it the potential for us to develop His characteristics and be conformed to His likeness.

In this lesson we will see that it is the Holy Spirit who regenerates us, and through Him we have the power to be everything that God wants us to be! He is the Spirit of Life who gives us eternal life and makes us joint heirs with our Savior, Jesus Christ.

lesson outline

The Convincing Spirit
The Spirit of Life
The Spirit of Adoption

lesson objectives

When you finish this lesson you should be able to:

- Describe the work of the Holy Spirit in convicting of sin and bringing repentance.
- Explain the results when the Holy Spirit gives life to a repentant sinner and dwells within him.
- Define the terms *sanctification of the Spirit* and *adoption by the Spirit.*
- Recognize privileges and responsibilities of those adopted into the family of God by the regenerating power of the Holy Spirit.

learning activities

1. As preparation for this lesson, reread the first two sections of Lesson 3: *He Convinces* and *He Regenerates.*

2. Study the lesson as instructed in the learning activities for Lesson 1. Read all Scriptures given and answer all of the study questions.

3. Take the self-test and check your answers.

key words

Abba	partakers	resistance
conform	perish	sanctification
glorified	prophesying	sanctify
heirs	repentance	transgressions

lesson development

THE CONVINCING SPIRIT

Bringing Conviction

Objective 1. *From given Scriptures, state possible results of the convicting power of the Holy Spirit.*

In Lesson 3 we saw that the Holy Spirit was sent into the world to convict the world of guilt in regard to sin, righteousness, and judgment. Turn back to Lesson 3 now and reread the first two sections, *He Convinces* and *He Regenerates,* as background for this lesson.

The Spirit alone can convince a sinner of his need for God. David, under the convicting power of the Holy Spirit, prayed, "For I know my transgressions, and my sin is always before me. Against you, you only, have I sinned and done what is evil in your sight" (Psalm 51:3-4).

The Spirit often uses human witnesses to speak to sinners. Here are some examples from Scripture:

1. *Peter.* On the Day of Pentecost, the great outpouring promised by Jesus had just taken place. Peter, who was full of the Holy Spirit, stood up and preached the gospel of Jesus Christ to the crowd that had gathered. His sermon is found in Acts 2:14-36.

When the crowd heard the words of Peter, they were "cut to the heart" (v. 37). Peter preached under the anointing of the Holy Spirit, and it was the convicting power of the Holy Spirit which reached the hearts of the people and caused them to ask, "Brothers, what shall we do?"

2. *Paul.* In his letter to the Corinthians, the apostle Paul tells them what will happen when an unbeliever comes into a meeting where everyone is prophesying under the anointing power of the Holy Spirit. Paul says, "he will be convinced by all that he is a sinner and will be judged by all, and the secrets of his heart will be laid bare. So he will fall down and worship God, exclaiming, 'God is really among you!'" (1 Corinthians 14:24-25).

3. *Stephen.* One of the first deacons chosen by the apostles was Stephen, "a man full of faith and of the Holy Spirit" (Acts 6:5). Stephen did many great and miraculous wonders among the people, and Jewish leaders began to oppose him. Acts 6:9-10 records that "These men began to argue with Stephen, but they could not stand up against his wisdom or the Spirit by which he spoke."

Acts chapter 7 contains the sermon Stephen preached to the Sanhedrin. The convicting power of the Holy Spirit was strong, as revealed in these concluding words of Stephen: "'You stiff-necked people, with uncircumcised hearts and ears! . . . You always resist the Holy Spirit!'" (v. 51).

1 What happened in response to Peter's sermon (Acts 2:41)?

....

....

2 Did everyone in Peter's audience respond in repentance to the convicting power of the Holy Spirit?

....

....

3 What happened in response to Stephen's sermon (Acts 7:54-60)?

....

....

Although the apostle Paul was well educated, he told the Corinthians, "My message and my preaching were not with wise and persuasive words, but with a demonstration of the Spirit's power so that your faith might not rest on men's wisdom but on God's power" (1 Corinthians 2:4-5). Paul had learned by experience to depend fully on the Holy Spirit's convicting power to bring men to Christ.

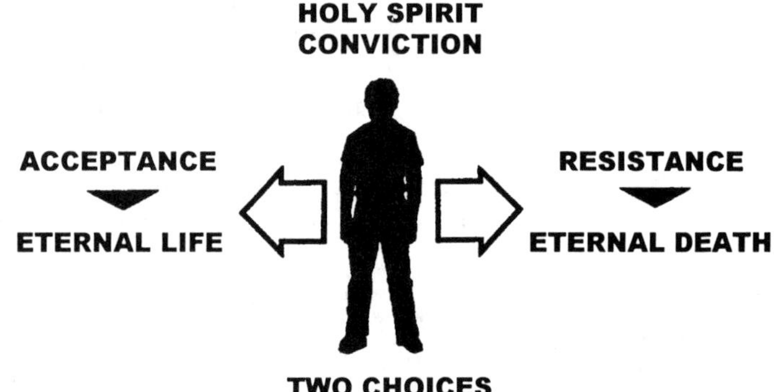

Bringing Repentance

Objective 2. *From examples given, distinguish true statements regarding the meaning of repentance and the Holy Spirit's part in bringing people to repentance.*

The Spirit alone can convince a sinner of his need for God, but He does not force the sinner to repent. Repentance requires an act of faith on the part of the sinner as he responds to the Holy Spirit's conviction. Paul told the Corinthians:

> Godly sorrow brings repentance that leads to salvation and leaves no regret (2 Corinthians 7:10).

This is the kind of sorrow expressed by the Psalmist David in Psalm 51:3-4. Godly sorrow causes the sinner to see himself as God sees him. It is the Spirit of God who reveals to him how God sees him (1 Corinthians 2:11).

What Is Repentance?

Repentance is the act in which one recognizes sin, turns from it, confesses it to God, and forsakes it completely. Repentance affects every part of us: intellect (or mind), emotions (or feelings), and will (expressed in behavior). Repentance is thus a changing of your mind, attitude, and behavior toward sin. It includes the knowledge of the wrong you have done and godly sorrow and grief over the dishonor it has brought to God. It is not merely a deep regret for sin or a promise not to do it again, but it is self-judgment in the presence of a righteous God. This can never happen without an awakening of the conscience to sin and a decision to turn away from sin, prompted by the Holy Spirit.

1. *Change of mind.* This change of mind comes from a *recognition* that one is not right with God. It results from the *knowledge* that he is headed in the wrong direction—that the consequences of this course will prove fatal. Seeing the awfulness of his situation, the prodigal son recognized what he had done and decided, "I will set out and go back to my father" (Luke 15:17-19). Included in repentance is the recognition that Jesus Christ is the only solution to one's sin problem. It is only through faith in Christ that we can have freedom from the guilt of sin.

2. *Change of feelings.* A realization of his sinful condition brings a feeling of sorrow to the sinner. Paul talked about this in his second letter to the Corinthians: ". . . now I am made happy, not because you were made sorry, but because your sorrow led

you to repentance. For you became sorrowful as God [the Holy Spirit] intended and so were not harmed in any way by us" (2 Corinthians 7:9). David expressed his emotion in Psalm 38:18 when he said, "I confess my iniquity; I am troubled by my sin." Regardless of the extent of grief one feels or expresses, the essential thing is confessing one's sins and deciding to forsake them. No amount of emotion will make up for confessing and forsaking sin.

3. *Change of behavior.* While it is important to *recognize* and *confess* sin, it is equally important *to turn away from it, forsaking it completely.* It was not enough for the prodigal to *recognize* his awful plight and feel bad about it. The moment of truth in his experience of repentance came when, through an act of the will, "He got up and went to his father" (Luke 15:20). Repentance involves every part of our life. It means not only *recognition* of sins and *sorrow* over the past but also our intentions for the future. It is the forsaking of our own way to go God's way in obedience and fellowship with Him.

Who Should Repent?

The call to repentance is universal. "God has overlooked the times when people did not know him, but now he commands *all of them everywhere to turn away from their evil ways*" (Acts 17:30, TEV). Every person is included in this call. All those who have never believed in Christ are invited to repent, receive God's forgiveness, and become a part of His family (John 3:15-17; Titus 2:11; Revelation 22:17).

The message of repentance is also for those who have believed in Christ and become His followers. While believers have been changed and are no longer controlled by sin, on occasion they may neglect their spiritual responsibilities, or not respond as they should to the Holy Spirit's direction for their spiritual development, or commit a sinful act (compare Romans 8:5-11 with Ephesians 4:17-32). Whatever the problem, repentance is the only solution for failure and sin. God's promise of forgiveness is directed primarily to Christians in 1 John 1:9, but it can be applied to anyone who is ready to repent. In chapters 2 and 3 of Revelation the call to repentance was repeated to five of seven churches addressed. These five churches were told by the Holy Spirit to repent or lose their witness, repent or be judged, repent or suffer tribulation, repent or suffer loss, and repent or be cast out. The exhortation "He who has an ear, let him hear what the Spirit says to the churches" (2:7) is repeated seven times in chapters 2 and 3, emphasizing the importance of listening to the Holy Spirit when He speaks and of heeding His message.

4 In this exercise, match the church and message of repentance from the Holy Spirit (right) to the reason repentance was necessary (left). (See Revelation 2 and 3.)

.... **a** *You tolerate that woman Jezebel,* whose teaching misleads my servants into immorality.	1) Church in Ephesus: "Repent and do the things you did at first."
.... **b** *You are dead ... I have not found your deeds complete in the sight of my God.*	2) Church in Pergamum "Repent therefore! Otherwise I will ... fight against them with the sword of my mouth."
.... **c** *You have lost your first love.*	3) Church in Thyatira: "I will make those who sin suffer intensely, unless they repent."
.... **d** *You are lukewarm —neither hot nor cold.*	4) Church in Sardis: "Wake up! If you do not wake up, I will come like a thief . . . ."
.... **e** *You have followed after false teachers.*	5) Church in Laodicea: "Those whom I love I rebuke and discipline, So be earnest, and repent."

Repentance brings forgiveness for one sin or for many (Matthew 18:21-22). God cannot tolerate sin. The measure of God's forgiveness is not determined by the kind or number of sins committed, but on sincere repentance—a change of mind, feeling, and behavior regarding sin. The time for repentance is *now*. The Holy Spirit, we have seen, is constantly convicting sinners to repent of their disobedience to God and to surrender their lives to Him. The Spirit is also at work in believers' lives entreating them to let Him have complete control of their lives and to keep in step with Him (Galatians 5:16-18, 25).

The opposite of repentance is resistance to the entreaties of the Holy Spirit. Stephen's message to the Jews, which we discussed earlier in this lesson, brought resistance and anger. This shows that it is possible for people who spend their whole lives in religion to resist the Holy Spirit (Acts 7:51). A review of Hebrews 10:26-31; Revelation 3:16, 19; and Proverbs 29:1 indicates that God loves man and willingly disciplines him to correct his misdeeds and conform him to the likeness of Christ. If he resists God's overtures and deliberately keeps on sinning, the only alternative is judgment: dreadful and final.

An illustration of this is someone calling you by telephone. If you continue to ignore ring after ring, he may eventually hang up the phone and quit trying to reach you. If you resist the Holy Spirit time after time, He may eventually stop trying to speak to your heart and call you to repentance. If you have unconfessed sins, *now* is the time to repent and receive full forgiveness.

5 Circle the letter preceding each TRUE statement concerning repentance and the Holy Spirit's part in bringing repentance.

a Repentance is a feeling of guilt for something you have done.

b The Holy Spirit's function in bringing the sinner to repentance is to cause him to see himself as God sees him, which produces godly sorrow.

c The sinner must change his mind, his feelings, and his behavior—this is what it means to repent.

d After salvation there is no further need for repentance.

e The message of the Holy Spirit to the seven churches in the book of Revelation was directed primarily to unbelievers.

f God's forgiveness is based on sincere repentance.

g It is possible to resist the Holy Spirit's convicting power to the point that He may eventually withdraw it from you.

THE SPIRIT OF LIFE

Giving New Birth

Objective 3. *From given Scriptures explain what happens when the Holy Spirit gives life to the sinner.*

When Nicodemus visited Jesus one night, Jesus told him he needed another birth (John 3:1-12). Nicodemus immediately thought of his natural birth, and asked, "How can a man be born when he is old?" (v. 4). Then Jesus explained that He was speaking of a spiritual birth, saying, "Flesh gives birth to flesh, but the Spirit gives birth to spirit" (v. 6). In other words, if one would enter God's kingdom, he must have this kind of spiritual birth.

Adam, the first man, had been given spiritual life in the beginning, but he sinned and lost it. By Adam's sin, Paul tells us, death came to all men, not only because of Adam's sin, but because all are guilty of sin (Romans 5:12).

In Paul's letter to the Ephesians, he says, "As for you, you were dead in your transgressions and sins" (Ephesians 2:1). But he goes on to say, "For it is by grace you have been saved, through faith" (v. 8). The reason, then, that everybody must be born again to enter God's kingdom is that all sinners are spiritually dead.

We have already seen that the Holy Spirit brings repentance by showing the sinner his need for the pardoning grace of God. As the sinner responds, confessing his sins and accepting God's salvation, the Spirit of life brings new life—spiritual life—to him. We say that the sinner has been *born again,* that is, he has experienced spiritual birth. What a wonderful change! Now he has the Holy Spirit of God within him, and he is free from the burden of guilt and sin.

There is no other way to become a Christian. Anything apart from this work of the Spirit of God is the effort of the flesh, and Jesus said that flesh can only give birth to flesh. Without the help of the Holy Spirit, it is impossible for spiritual change to take place in a person's life.

6 Read each of the following Scriptures and write what each says about the activity of the Holy Spirit in giving spiritual life to the repentant sinner:

a John 6:63 ....

b Romans 8:2 ....

c Galatians 4:4-6 ....

d Galatians 5:16-18, 25 ....

These Scriptures reveal that it is the Holy Spirit who imparts spiritual life. All we have to do is cooperate and accept this gift of life.

7 Read Romans 8:1-11 and fill in the blanks.

a When you are set free from the law of sin and death by the Holy Spirit, you no longer live according to the sinful nature, but according to the ....

b When you live in accordance with the Spirit, your mind is set on what the Spirit ....

c The only way to please God is to be controlled by the. ....

d If anyone does not have the Spirit of Christ, he does not belong to ....

I AM GOD'S TEMPLE

Everyone who is born of God receives the Spirit of God. "The Spirit himself testifies with our spirit that we are God's children" (Romans 8:16). This is what God had in mind from the very beginning. He wants man to be His temple, His dwelling place. Paul reminded the Corinthians of this: "Don't you know that you yourselves are God's temple and that God's Spirit lives in you?" (1 Corinthians 3:16).

In Romans 8:9 the Holy Spirit is called the *Spirit of Christ,* and rightly so, because He represents Christ in us. He was given by the Father to be with us in Christ's stead. Paul also calls the

Holy Spirit the *Spirit of His Son* (Galatians 4:6). That is why he could also say, "Christ lives in me" (Galatians 2:20).

Dwelling Within Us

Objective 4. *Select true statements concerning the indwelling Spirit in the life of a Christian.*

When Jesus said of the Spirit, "He lives with you and *will be* in you" (John 14:17), His disciples apparently did not grasp the significance of the statement. The apostle Paul speaks to the issue, stating that such a privilege requires responsible living on the part of each believer (John 14:16-17; 1 Corinthians 3:16-17; 6:19-20; 2 Corinthians 6:16-17). He emphasizes this in Romans 8:12-17, where he says, we have an obligation to put to death the misdeeds of the body (vs. 12-13). Recognition of the Spirit's control over our lives brings *awareness* of our sonship (vs, 15-16) and of our future spiritual inheritance (v. 17). The idea of the Holy Spirit living within me means that He is there all the time. This gives consistency to my relationship with Him. He is not just a divine visitor; He has taken up full-time residency in me. Let's summarize briefly the benefits that are ours as a result of the indwelling Spirit.

Part of the function of the indwelling Spirit is to act as our counselor and teacher. In this capacity, He enables us to grasp the truth and He instructs us concerning the teaching of Jesus, bringing His teaching to our minds (John 14:26; 16:13-15). The indwelling Spirit helps us in our weakness and intercedes for us according to the will of God (Romans 8:26-27).

> One of the most important aspects of the Spirit's work in the believer is related to an experience which takes place *after* the believer has experienced the new birth. It is referred to as the baptism with or in the Holy Spirit (we will discuss this in depth in Lesson 7). Jesus told the Twelve shortly before His ascension that they were to stay in the city until they were clothed with power from on high (Luke 24:49). A bit later He clarified this: "Do not leave Jerusalem, but wait for the

gift my Father promised ... in a few days you will be baptized with the Holy Spirit" (Acts 1:4-5). Following this baptism with the Spirit, Jesus said His followers would receive power to be witnesses not only in their own lands but also throughout the whole world (Acts 1:8). The book of Acts records the truth of Jesus' statement, for Spirit-filled believers became a powerful instrument for evangelism throughout the world.

Also associated with the Spirit baptism is the development of spiritual gifts. The apostle Paul refers to spiritual gifts in Romans 12:4-8; 1 Corinthians 12 and 14; and Ephesians 4:11-16. These gifts serve to edify and build up the body of Christ. (We will discuss these in depth in Lesson 9.)

Finally, as the Spirit dwells within He produces spiritual fruit, which some see as the development of Christian character (Galatians 5:16-25). Spiritual fruit is contrasted with the works of the sinful nature and results from living by and keeping in step with the Spirit. (We will discuss the fruit of the Spirit more fully in Lesson 10.)

8 Based on the Scriptures we have discussed in this section, which of the following statements are TRUE?

a Although the sinner does not realize it, the Holy Spirit dwells within him because he is a temple of God.

b Now that the Holy Spirit has begun to dwell within you, you have an obligation to bring your manner of life into conformity with His desires.

c The Holy Spirit's indwelling brings His assistance as Counselor, Teacher, and Intercessor.

d The Holy Spirit baptism is given primarily to empower believers to witness effectively for their risen Lord.

e The gifts of the Spirit serve to build up the body of Christ.

f The fruit of the Spirit results from the good intentions of believers to make themselves acceptable models of the Christian faith.

Sanctifying Us

Objective 5. *Identify correct explanations of "sanctification by the Holy Spirit."*

Another work of the indwelling Spirit is to *sanctify* us. In its simplest form, *sanctification* means that the Holy Spirit makes the believer holy by separating him from sin and setting him apart for God. This happens as the believer submits himself totally to the guidance of the Spirit so that the control of sin is stripped from his life (Romans 8:2, 9).

Paul speaks of the Gentiles becoming an offering acceptable to God, *sanctified by the Holy Spirit* (Romans 15:16). He tells the Corinthians they were washed, justified, and sanctified in the name of the Lord Jesus Christ and *by the Spirit of our God* (1 Corinthians 6:11). To the church in Thessalonica he writes these words:

> But we ought always to thank God for you, brothers loved by the Lord, because from the beginning God chose you to be saved through the sanctifying work of the Spirit and through belief in the truth. He called you to this through our gospel, that you might share in the glory of our Lord Jesus Christ (2 Thessalonians 2:13-14).

When we experience the new birth, the Holy Spirit makes us acceptable to God and we stand before Him on the basis of Christ's completed work of redemption. We are declared righteous and our position before God is just as if we had never sinned. Yet, we must work out in practice what has been declared. We are newly born spiritual infants, and we are admonished to grow and mature (2 Peter 3:18; 2 Timothy 2:15; 1 Peter 2:2-3). Thus, the work of the Holy Spirit in us has just begun. Being spiritually alive, we have the ability to respond to God. We are destined for eternal life, and en route to that goal we are admonished to mature and develop in Christlikeness. We are to be the copy of the One who has saved us and whose seed remains in us (1 John 3:9). As we have seen in our consideration of Romans 8:5-16, Galatians 5:16-25, and Ephesians 4:20-32, the putting off of the old self and the putting on of the new self is a progressive work that has as its goal the development of the image of Christ in each of us (Romans 8:29). Now, with the help of the Holy Spirit, we must learn daily to separate ourselves from the things which He shows us are not pleasing to God. Progressively we are being conformed to His image. One day we shall be like Him, for we shall see Him just as He is (1 John 3:2). Until then, we endeavor to be ever more sensitive to the Spirit's control; we are in the process of being perfected.

SEPARATION = SANCTIFICATION

9 Choose the correct completions: *Sanctification by the Spirit* means that we

a) are made instantaneously perfect and cannot sin henceforth.
b) have been set apart unto God and from sin.
c) are daily being conformed to the image of Christ by allowing the Holy Spirit to direct us in all that we do.
d) allow the Spirit to help us do the things that are pleasing to God.

THE SPIRIT OF ADOPTION

Objective 6. *Examine your own experience of regeneration and the work of the Spirit of adoption in your life.*

Making Us Heirs

> Therefore, brothers, we have an obligation-but it is not to the sinful nature, to live according to it. For if you live according to the sinful nature, you will die; but if by the Spirit you put to death the misdeeds of the body, you will live, because those who are led by the Spirit of God are sons of God. For you did not receive a spirit that makes you a slave again to fear, but you received the Spirit of sonship [adoption]. And by him we cry, "Abba, Father." The Spirit himself testifies with our spirit that we are God's children. Now if we are children, then we are heirs—heirs of God and co-heirs with Christ, if indeed we share in his sufferings in order that we may also share in his glory (Romans 8:12-17).

What does the apostle Paul mean in these verses when he calls the Holy Spirit the *Spirit of adoption?* Adoption concerns a person's *position* in the family of God and concerns his *privileges* as one of God's sons. One aspect of adoption for the Romans referred to a child who was legally adopted into a family. Often poor parents who could not provide adequately for their child would give him over for adoption by a wealthy family. The adoptive parents were given full control of the child, and the child was given the same rights in the family as any of the other children; however, during their minority (before they came of legal age) all the children (natural and adoptive) differed little from household servants (Galatians 4:1-2). The full benefits of sonship were deferred until they came of age.

By means of the new birth the Holy Spirit, who is the Spirit of life, makes us actual partakers of the nature of God. Then, by the Spirit of adoption, we are given immediate standing in the family of God. This means that all of the privileges normally associated with family membership are ours. However, in contrast to the Roman system, we don't have "deferred benefits" that must await our coming of age. Rather, through His act of adoption God places us in His family in the rank or position of adult sons (Galatians 4:1-7). Thus, we have all the privileges of being sons and are regarded as true sons.

Paul refers to this positional aspect of adoption in his letter to the Galatians. (See Galatians 3:26-29 and 4:1-7.) Children, he says, are no different from the servants, even though they are the heirs of everything. They are subject to guardians and trustees until the time appointed by the father. Then they are placed as adult sons. He tells the Galatians, who are acting like children under the bondage of the old Jewish ordinances, that they have received *full rights as sons.* He continues, "Because you are sons, God sent the Spirit of his Son into our hearts, the Spirit who calls out, 'Abba, Father.' So you are no longer a slave, but a son; and since you are a son, God has made you also an heir" (Galatians 4:6-7).

One of the immediate benefits of our adult status as adoptive sons is the inner spiritual assurance that we are God's sons. The Spirit testified to this when we received Him (Romans 8:12-17; 1 John 3:24; 4:13-14), and because of this witness we are able to call Him *Father.* John reinforces this teaching, noting that *now* we are the children of God (1 John 3:2). No one must await Christ's coming or future judgment to determine his spiritual status. Having received Christ as his Savior, he has both the inner witness of the Spirit and the external witness of the Word of God that he is a son of God.

While we are now sons of God with all the rights and privileges of adult heirs, we yet await a full realization of sonship when we stand in God's presence and receive our glorified bodies. Paul affirms this in Romans 8:23 when he says, "We ourselves, who have the first fruits of the Spirit, groan inwardly as we wait eagerly for our adoption as sons, the redemption of our bodies."

This is further explained by the apostle John in 1 John 3:2: "Dear friends, now we are children of God, and what we will be has not yet been made known. But we know that when he [Jesus] appears, we shall be like him, for we shall see him as he is."

John later says that "anyone who does not do what is right is not a child of God; neither is anyone who does not love his brother" (1 John 3:10, 21-24; 5:1-3). Being apart of the family of God carries with it certain responsibilities as well as privileges. It is the Spirit of God within you who makes it possible for you to fulfill these responsibilities. He puts divine love in your heart and gives you a desire to do those things which please your heavenly Father.

10 Based upon our discussion in this section, choose the best answer. The term *Spirit of adoption* refers to
a) the act of the Holy Spirit by which I become a child of God at the time of regeneration.
b) the Holy Spirit's right to place me in the position He chooses in relation to other believers.
c) the Holy Spirit's complete control over the believer the moment he experiences new birth.

11 Adoption into the family of God takes place when I
a) receive my glorified body.
b) cry out, "Abba, Father."
c) experience the new birth.

12 From the following Scriptures, name three ways you can know that you are a child of God, that you have been born again of the Spirit (Romans 8:16; 1 John 3:10, 21-24; 4:13-14; 5:1-3).

....

....

13 Examine yourself by writing *yes* or *no* in the blank spaces below.

a I have repented of my sins............................

b By faith I have accepted Jesus Christ as my personal Savior............................

c I know that even though I am a Christian, I need to repent for occasional failures and receive forgiveness ....

d I know that repentance means turning away from sin and toward God ....

e Because I have been set free from the law of sin and death, I want to do what the Spirit desires ....

f I want the Holy Spirit to sanctify me and make me more like Jesus every day ....

g I know that I am a Christian because I have the witness of God's Word and the witness of God's Spirit within. ....

h I realize that adoption into the family of God gives me certain responsibilities as well as rights ....

This might be a good time to meditate on each of these statements and determine whether you have experienced all that is available to you in Christ. Ask the Holy Spirit to make real to you your place in God's family, with all the rights and duties that are yours as a child of God.

self-test

ALTERNATE CHOICE. For each subject below two statements are made. Select the statement which is most complete and accurate based on this lesson. Circle the letter preceding your choice.

1 *Regeneration:*

a) This is a work of the Holy Spirit in which He brings new spiritual life to the repentant sinner who confesses his sin and accepts Jesus Christ as Savior.

b) This is a change of mind and feeling regarding one's spiritual condition, and a desire to live a life free from sin.

2 *Conviction*:

a) The convicting power of the Holy Spirit is so strong that a sinner has no choice but to respond to it by turning away from his sin and obeying God. It is often accompanied by feelings of guilt and by recognition that it is impossible to live a sinless life.

b) While the Holy Spirit often convicts a sinner directly and convinces him of his need for God, He often works through an anointed public message or a personal witness to speak to the sinner's heart.

3 *Repentance*:

a) Repentance is godly sorrow which makes the sinner see himself as he really is. He recognizes that he must change his ways if he wants to have eternal life, and he tries to stop doing the things that will lead to eternal death.

b) Repentance involves a change of mind regarding sin, a change of feeling which includes sincere sorrow for a sinful life, and a change of behavior which includes turning away from sin and toward God. There is inward change as well as outward change. The sinner must repent of sins in order to receive God's salvation; the believer must repent of any failure or shortcoming that may hinder his spiritual development toward Christlikeness.

4 *Results of spiritual life:*

a) I am set free from the temptations of the devil so that I am no longer bothered by the desire to do sinful things.

b) I no longer live according to the sinful nature, but my mind is set on what the Holy Spirit wants me to do.

5 *The indwelling Spirit:*

a) When the Holy Spirit takes up residence within me, I receive many personal benefits. He makes my sonship real, He helps me pray appropriately, and He convicts me of misdeeds and helps me overcome them.

b) When the Holy Spirit dwells within me and makes my body His temple, He takes complete control, so that all of my choices, actions, and thoughts are really His choices, actions, and thoughts. I am no longer bothered by human needs and desires because He takes all of that from me.

6 *Sanctification by the Spirit:*

a) As I yield myself to the Holy Spirit's control, He enables me to separate myself from sin and unto God. This is a progressive work which conforms me to the image of Christ as I yield to the Holy Spirit and allow Him to develop in me the fruit of the Spirit.

b) This is a special act of the Holy Spirit in which I am suddenly conformed to the image of Christ and given the fruit of the Spirit.

7 *The Spirit of adoption:*

a) When I reach full Christian maturity, I am considered worthy of adoption into the family of God, with all the rights and responsibilities of an heir. It is the Holy Spirit who determines when I am ready for adoption and witnesses to my heart that I am a child of God.

b) When the Holy Spirit gives me new birth, He makes me an actual partaker of the nature of God. He also adopts me into God's family, giving me the full rights of sonship, and I become a joint heir with Jesus Christ of all of the privileges of the children of God. I know that I am born again into the family of God because His Spirit witnesses to my spirit, because I want to do what is right, and because He gives me love for my brothers and sisters in Christ.

answers to study questions

7 a Spirit.
b desires.
c Spirit.
d Christ.

1 Many accepted his message and were baptized.

8 a False.
b True.
c True.
d True.
e True.
f False. (Spiritual fruit results from living by and keeping in step with the Spirit.)

2 No, the Scripture "Those who accepted his message" (2:41) implies that some resisted the Holy Spirit.

9 Answers b), c), and d) are correct.

3 Those who heard him became very angry and resisted the Spirit of God. They stoned Stephen until he was dead.

10 a) the act of the Holy Spirit by which I become a child of God at the time of regeneration.

4 a 3) Church in Thyatira.
b 4) Church in Sardis.
c 1) Church in Ephesus.
d 5) Church in Laodicea.
e 2) Church in Pergamum.

11 c) experience the new birth.

5 a False. (Repentance involves change.)
b True.
c True.
d False.
e False.
f True.
g True.

12 The Holy Spirit bears witness with my spirit. I will do what is right. I will love my brother (fellow Christians).

6 a The Spirit gives life.
b The law of the Spirit of life sets me free from the law of sin and death.
c The Spirit gives substance to our spiritual life and makes our sonship real.
d We live by the Spirit and we are led in acceptable Christian living.

13 Your answer. I hope you were able to answer *yes* to each statement.

LESSON 7

THE SPIRIT WHO EMPOWERS

Teaching in a Bible college has always been exiting for me as I watch the Holy Spirit work in the lives of the students. The transforming work He performs in the lives of students never ceases to amaze me!

Many students come to Bible school with what seems to be little talent for public ministry; however, they generally come with a conviction that God has called them. Then as they study, pray, and give themselves to the Holy Spirit, a miracle gradually takes place. As the Holy Spirit comes to control them more fully, anoint their yielded native talents, and enlighten their minds through systematic study, all kinds of abilities begin to emerge. As a bud gradually opens up to the morning dew and the rising sun to become a beautiful, fully-developed flower, these students develop in the Spirit from day to day. By the time graduation arrives, they are ready for the ministry to which God has called them. They leave the school and go out to become successful pastors, evangelists, or missionaries.

This enablement of the Spirit has been in evidence from the time God called His first witnesses. While some, such as the apostle Paul, were highly educated, many of the greatest among them came from very humble beginnings. Whatever the background, training, or native abilities of the human vessels, the factor which helped them turn the world upside down was not human eloquence or superior wisdom but the demonstration of the Spirit's power (1 Corinthians 2:1-5).

In this lesson you will learn that when the Holy Spirit comes into your life in baptismal fullness, He will help you to be an effective worker in the kingdom of God. The same power that was available to Old Testament men of God and New Testament disciples is available for you today!

lesson outline

Old Testament Characters
New Testament Disciples
Twentieth-Century Believers

lesson objectives

When you finish this lesson you should be able to:

- Give examples from the Old Testament of the Holy Spirit's anointing in the lives of men chosen by God.
- Describe the change in New Testament disciples after the outpouring of the Holy Spirit on the Day of Pentecost and results of the change.
- Relate the modern-day outpouring of the Spirit to the purpose of world evangelization and hastening the coming of the Lord.

learning activities

1. Study the lesson as instructed in the learning activities for Lesson 1. Read all Scripture texts indicated and answer all of the study questions.
2. Take the self-test and check your answers.
3. Review Lessons 4-7 and then answer the questions in Unit Student Report 2.

key words

accomplishments	enduement	pentecostal
charismatic	fulfillment	presumptuous
concentration	impulsive	receptive
confirms	indwelling	recipient
contradictions	infilling	spontaneous
empowering	Pentateuch	

lesson development

OLD TESTAMENT CHARACTERS

In the Pentateuch

Objective 1. *State the purpose for which God sent the Holy Spirit upon chosen men during the time described in the Pentateuch.*

Pentateuch is the name given to the first five books of the Old Testament: Genesis, Exodus, Leviticus, Numbers, and Deuteronomy. They are often called "the books of Moses" since it is commonly accepted that Moses is the human author of these five books.

The accent on the Holy Spirit in these five books, and in all of the Old Testament, is definitely more on what He *does* than what He *is*. The Old Testament says practically nothing about the personality of the Holy Spirit, but it is filled with miraculous works of the Spirit, beginning with creative acts in Genesis 1.

The emphasis in the Old Testament is on the Holy Spirit's *coming upon men* for a specific service to be performed. The indwelling presence of the Holy Spirit, however, is a New Testament phenomenon. This is confirmed in the words of John: "Up to that time the Spirit had not been given, since Jesus had not yet been glorified" (John 7:39), and the words of Jesus when He was speaking of the coming Holy Spirit: "But you know him, for he lives with you and will be in you" (John 14:17).

By way of comparison, we can say that, on the basis of biblical evidence, Old Testament personalities enjoyed the occasional presence of the Holy Spirit on their lives to enable them to accomplish specific tasks to which God assigned them; whereas, New Testament believers enjoy the indwelling presence of the Holy Spirit on a permanent basis. First, the Spirit comes to the believer as the agent of regeneration. Then, as we shall see (Matthew 3:11; Mark 1:8; John 1:33; Acts 1:5), believers are baptized into the Holy Spirit and receive Him in baptismal fullness.

The Holy Spirit began to deal with men immediately after the Fall. He found men like Noah, Abraham, Isaac, and even Jacob who were receptive to His dealings. Even though little is said specifically about the Holy Spirit in references to these men, we know they were led by Him as they were obedient to God. God's Spirit works in the lives of men without drawing attention to Himself. His *work* is often seen in the Old Testament even when He is not mentioned by name.

There are also, in the Old Testament, specific references to the work of the Holy Spirit in the lives of men. Who are some of the others used mightily by the Holy Spirit in the Pentateuch?

1. *Joseph* is the first mentioned as a man "in whom is the Spirit of God" (Genesis 41:38). Pharaoh recognized this quality

in Joseph because of his supernatural ability to interpret dreams. The Spirit of God in or upon Joseph enabled him to resist temptation and become the overseer of an entire nation.

2. *Moses* was chosen by God to lead the Israelites out of Egypt. Isaiah tells that Moses was God's shepherd of Israel, and that God "set his Holy Spirit among them" (Isaiah 63:11). Isaiah further reports that "they were given rest by the Spirit of the Lord" (Isaiah 63:14).

When it was time to build a tabernacle for the Lord, God spoke to Moses and told him He had chosen a foreman for the job, saying "I have filled him with the Spirit of God, with skill, ability, and knowledge in all kinds of crafts" (Exodus 31:2-3). The foreman was given divine ability in all the skills necessary to build the Lord's house.

When Moses became overwhelmed by the burdens of his people and complained to God, the Lord gave the Holy Spirit to seventy elders to assist Moses in meeting the needs of the people.

1 Read Numbers 11:10-17 and 24-25 and answer these questions:

a What verse indicates that the Holy Spirit was upon Moses?

....

b What method did God use to give the Holy Spirit to the seventy elders?

....

c As the Spirit rested on these seventy elders, what did they all do? ....

3. *Joshua* was chosen by the Lord to be the successor of Moses. The Lord said to Moses: "Take Joshua . . . a man in whom is the spirit [or Spirit] and lay your hand on him" (Numbers 27:18). It was in the power of the Spirit that Joshua was able to lead his people to take possession of the Promised Land. At the beginning of his period of leadership this was written of him: "Now Joshua son of Nun was filled with the

spirit [or Spirit] of wisdom because Moses had laid his hands on him" (Deuteronomy 34:9). So from Egypt to Canaan, Israel was led by leaders empowered by the Holy Spirit.

While it may on occasion seem to be helpful to say that the Spirit was *on* Old Testament personalities and *in* New Testament believers, this device does not solve the difference satisfactorily. Biblical evidence indicates that it is better to say that in the Old Testament the Spirit's enablement was selective and occasional whereas in the New Testament it is general and permanent. It is evident that each of the foregoing examples indicates a long-term need for and experience of the Spirit's enablement.

2 State the purpose for which God sent the Holy Spirit to rest upon each of the men listed below:

a Joseph ....

b Moses ....

c The seventy elders ....

d Joshua ....

e Based upon the evidence given in each of the above cases, was the Spirit's enablement a short-term or a long-term experience?

....

LED BY THE HOLY SPIRIT

In the Historical Books

Objective 2. *State a principle that can be learned from the lives of Samson, Saul, and David.*

The book of Joshua records the many victories of the Israelites as they moved into Canaan under Joshua's leadership and took possession of the land Joshua's Spirit-anointed leadership can be summed up by what is written in Joshua 24:31:

> Israel served the Lord throughout the lifetime of Joshua and of the elders who outlived him and who had experienced everything the Lord had done for Israel.

Judges 2: 10-12 tells what happened next:

> After that whole generation had been gathered to their fathers, another generation grew up, who knew neither the Lord nor what he had done for Israel. Then the Israelites did evil in the eyes of the Lord and served the Baals. They forsook the Lord, the God of their fathers, who had brought them out of Egypt

As a result of this, the judgment of the Lord came upon them, and He allowed the Israelites to be overcome by their enemies whenever they went out to fight. Judges 2:16 tells us, "Then the Lord raised up judges."

During the times of the judges the power of the Holy Spirit was especially apparent. There were many failures on the part of those who were chosen to deliver God's people from the cruelty of their enemies, but God used the judges in spite of their weaknesses.

Altogether there were 13 judges who ruled Israel over a period of about 300 years. The stories of *Gideon* and *Samson* tell of humanly impossible accomplishments as the Spirit of the Lord came upon them.

3 Read Judges 6:11-15. When the Lord appeared to Gideon, what kind of man did Gideon describe himself as being?

....

Because Gideon was obedient to the instructions of the angel of the Lord, the Spirit of the Lord came upon him (Judges 6:34); God used Gideon to deliver Israel from the innumerable forces of Midian with only 300 selected men.

Samson is a lesson to all who would take the Spirit of God for granted in their life and ministry for God. He was prepared to lead Israel even before his birth (see Judges chapters 13-16). when he was still a young boy, "the Lord blessed him, and the Spirit of the Lord began to stir him" (Judges 13:24-25).

4 Read Judges 14:6, 19; and 15:14. What is written about Samson in all of these verses?

....

Samson was set apart unto God from birth, and God chose him to deliver Israel from the Philistines. However, Samson was not obedient to his vow unto the Lord.

5 Read Judges 16:15-20. What happened when Samson broke his vow and revealed the source of his strength?

....

....

When the people of Israel insisted on a man for their king (1 Samuel 8:4-5), God gave them Saul. The prophet Samuel told Saul, "The Spirit of the Lord will come upon you in power, and you will prophesy with them; and you will be changed into a different person" (1 Samuel 10:6). This prophecy was fulfilled that very day, and God used Saul mightily in the beginning of his career as king of Israel, but, like Samson, he did not continue to respect and obey God. Thus, the most tragic words that can be written of a person were written of him.

6 Read 1 Samuel 16:14. what are these tragic words?

....

At the same time, the Holy Spirit was preparing a young shepherd boy to become the king of Israel. The Scriptures ten how Samuel found him, took the horn of oil and anointed him, "and from that day on the Spirit of the Lord came upon David in power" (1 Samuel 16:13).

David is one of the few Old Testament characters upon whom the Spirit of the Lord rested continuously. His accomplishments would have been impossible without the omnipotent Holy Spirit who rested upon him.

David was very aware of the need for the Holy Spirit's presence in his life. When he had sinned, he repented, and cried out to God, "Do not cast me from your presence or take your Holy Spirit from me" (Psalm 51:11).

7 What principle can be learned from the failure of Samson, Saul, and David, concerning the presence of the Holy Spirit in their lives?

In the Prophets

Objective 3. *Recognize a statement which reflects the attitude of the Old Testament prophets concerning their need for the Holy Spirit in their lives.*

The Holy Spirit used the writing prophets to play a major role in the latter history of Israel. Their writings make up a significant portion of Old Testament Scripture.

The prophet *Micah* said of himself what could be said of all genuine prophets of God: "But as for me, I am filled with power, with the Spirit of the Lord" (Micah 3:8).

Ezekiel told how the Spirit lifted him up between the earth and heaven and took him in visions to Jerusalem (Ezekiel 8:3).

The Holy Spirit's presence in *Daniel* was recognized by the heathen king Nebuchadnezzar, who said to Daniel: "I know that the spirit of the holy gods is in you, and no mystery is too difficult for you" (Daniel 4:9).

New Testament writers were quick to recognize the anointing of the Holy Spirit on the prophets. Paul told the Jews at Rome, "The Holy Spirit spoke the truth to your forefathers when he said through *Isaiah* the prophet: . . ." (Acts 28:25).

The writer to the Hebrews quotes (10:15-17) Jeremiah 31:33-34, saying "The Holy Spirit also testifies about this . . . ." That is, the words from Jeremiah's writing were recognized as the words of the Holy Spirit.

The apostle Peter confirms the work of the Holy Spirit in the prophets by his words in 2 Peter 1:20-21:

> Above all, you must understand that no prophecy of Scripture came about by the prophet's own interpretation. For prophecy never had its origin in the will of man, but men spoke from God as they were carried along by the Holy Spirit.

8 Which of the following statements best reflects the attitude of the Old Testament prophets concerning their need for the Holy Spirit in their lives? Circle the letter preceding your choice.

a) David's request: "Do not cast me from your presence or take your Holy Spirit from me" (Psalm 51:11).
b) Zechariah's declaration: "'Not by might nor by power, but by my Spirit,' says the Lord Almighty" (Zechariah 4:6).
c) Micah's statement: "But as for me, I am filled with power, with the Spirit of the Lord" (Micah 3:8).

NEW TESTAMENT DISCIPLES

Objective 4. *Contrast and analyze the witness of the apostle Peter before and at Pentecost.*

Before Pentecost

The main concentration of the Holy Spirit in the New Testament prior to Pentecost was on the Person and work of Jesus. We have already discussed the ministry of Jesus in Lesson 5, in the section *The Living Word,* so we will not repeat it in this lesson.

A few New Testament people received a special enablement of the Holy Spirit prior to Pentecost for a specific purpose. They are:

1. John the Baptist (Luke 1:15)
2. Parents of John the Baptist (Luke 1:41, 67)
3. Mary, mother of Jesus (Matthew 1:18, 20)
4. Simeon (Luke 2:25)

The Holy Spirit did not work directly with the disciples except on special occasions when they were sent out by Jesus to minister. (See Matthew 10:1; Mark 3:13-15; Mark 6:7; Luke 9:1; and Luke 10:19). These Scriptures indicate that as Jesus sent the disciples out to minister, He gave them *authority* to do miracles in His name. Earlier we saw that He received His authority from the Holy Spirit. He gave this same authority to the disciples for the purpose of ministry.)

Most of the time, the disciples were with Jesus. He was their divine Teacher. They watched Him, listened to Him, and tried to imitate Him, but often they failed. He was able to be *with* them during that time, but not *in* them. They would not be able to fully share the power that rested on Him until after His death and resurrection. As the apostle John later wrote, "Up to that time the Spirit had not been given, since Jesus had not yet been glorified" (John 7:39).

The history of the disciples before and after Pentecost reminds me of advertisements which contrast how persons are *before* they use the product advertised and how they are *after* using the product. For example:

The weakling becomes a muscle-man.
The plain little maiden becomes a beautiful model.
The poor tenant farmer becomes a rich landlord.
The sweating laborer becomes a powerful manager.

The purpose of these advertisements is to convince people that they can experience the same success if they will use the product.

A study of the apostle Peter *before* and *after* Pentecost is convincing proof of the change in a person's life which takes place as a result of the infilling of the Holy Spirit. In this section we will consider what Peter was like *before* Pentecost.

PETER BEFORE PENTECOST

1. Impulsive (acted without thought)—Matthew 14:28; 17:4; John 21:7
2. Full of contradictions:
   a. Presumptuous—Matthew 16:22; John 13:8; 18:10
   Timid and cowardly—Matthew 14:30; 26:69-72
   b. Both self-seeking and self-sacrificing—Matthew 19:27; Mark 1:18
   c. Sometimes had spiritual insight and other times showed lack of understanding of spiritual truths—John 6:68; Matthew 15:15-16
   d. Made two confessions of faith in Christ—Matthew 16:16; John 6:69
   Was guilty of a cowardly denial of Christ—Mark 14:67-71
   Followed afar off—Matthew 26:58
3. Associated with evil men—John 18:18
4. Guilty of blasphemy—Mark 14:70-71

SHIFTING SAND

On the resurrection evening Jesus appeared to His disciples and gave them a preview of what was to come. He breathed on them and said, "Receive the Holy Spirit" (John 20:22). Many see in this command a reference to the work of the Spirit in regeneration, for He is the active agent in regeneration. This act confirmed that He had finished the work of restoring man to God. However, He did not at that time baptize them in the Holy Spirit. When Jesus met with them later, He referred to the baptism in the Holy Spirit as still to come (Acts 1:4, 8).

9 Which of these statements explains how the disciples were able to maintain their faith in Christ prior to Pentecost?
a) They studied the Scriptures and went to the temple daily to pray.
b) They had the presence of the Holy Spirit without the power.
c) They were with Jesus most of the time, learning from Him.

At Pentecost

Finally the day came that Jesus had promised. The sound of heavenly wind filled the upper room where the disciples and other believers were waiting. They saw what seemed to be tongues of fire that separated and came to rest on each of them. As they breathed in the divine presence, they were all filled with the Holy Spirit and began to speak in languages they had never learned. The Holy Spirit was giving them the words to say (Acts 2:1-4).

It was exactly as John the Baptist and Jesus had promised. They were being baptized in the Holy Spirit and fire (Matthew 3:11; Acts 1:5). Jesus had promised they would speak in new languages, and it was happening as they spoke the words the Holy Spirit gave to them (Mark 16:17).

There were thousands of God-fearing Jews in Jerusalem from all the surrounding nations. They had come for the Feast of Pentecost. When they heard the sounds from the upper room, a great crowd gathered. The crowd was bewildered because each person heard someone speaking his own language. "Are not all these men who are speaking Galileans?" they asked. "Then how is it that each of us hears them in his own native language?" (Acts 2:7-8).

Some made fun of them and said they had taken too much wine, but Peter stood up and explained what had happened. He preached that Christ was alive and this was the fulfillment of His promise to send the Holy Spirit.

Many were convicted by the Holy Spirit and cried out, "What shall we do?" Peter answered, "Repent and be baptized, every one of you, in the name of Jesus Christ for the forgiveness of your sins. And you will receive the gift of the Holy Spirit" (Acts 2:37-38). Three thousand responded and were baptized. It was a great day for the church—in fact, in one sense, it was the day of its birth! (Acts 2:1-41).

10 Review Acts 1 and 2 again. Which of the disciples took leadership after the ascension of Christ?

....

After Pentecost

The power of Pentecost did not cease with the passing of the Day of Pentecost. That day was only the beginning of the age of special activity by the Holy Spirit. Through Christ's death and resurrection, the way had been opened for the Holy Spirit to come and live in the hearts of the believers.

The Day of Pentecost had brought the baptism in the Holy Spirit, that special enduement of power that Jesus promised would make them His effective witnesses. The success of the disciples after Pentecost is summarized in Hebrews 2:4: "God also testified to it by signs, wonders and various miracles, and gifts of the Holy Spirit distributed according to his will."

Peter is a good example of what happened *after Pentecost.* Compare this chart with the one *before Pentecost.*

PETER AFTER PENTECOST

1. Became a powerful preacher and leader in the early church—Acts chapters 1-5 and 10-12
2. Gave a powerful confession of Christ—John 1:42; Matthew 16:18; Acts 1:8
3. Performed miracles—Acts 3:7; 5:15; 9:34, 40
4. Was courageous and bold—Acts 4:19-20; 5:28-29, 40, 42
5. Was an encouragement and a good example to the suffering, early church—1 Peter
6. Gave instruction to the church concerning false teachers and scoffers—2 Peter

SOLID ROCK

If you compare this chart with our previous chart, you will see that the infilling of the Holy Spirit made the difference in Peter's ability to witness effectively for his Lord. Instead of cowardly denial he gave a powerful and effective witness to multitudes of Christ's saving grace.

PETER BEFORE . . .

"I KNOW HIM NOT"

AND AFTER

"JESUS IS LORD"

The revival which began in Jerusalem when Peter preached his powerful sermon on the Day of Pentecost was taken to Samaria by a Spirit-filled deacon named Philip. People believed the gospel message and were baptized in water. Many miracles took place; however, no one was baptized in the Holy Spirit. So Peter and John were sent down from Jerusalem. They laid hands on the new believers, who received the Holy Spirit (Acts 8:4-17).

The next recorded reception of the Holy Spirit was by the newly converted Saul of Tarsus, who became Paul. When Ananias prayed for him, Saul was filled with the Holy Spirit and became the great apostle to the Gentiles (Acts 9:17).

The first pentecostal contact with the Gentiles, however, was made by the apostle Peter. The Spirit sent Peter, against the apostle's will, to the house of Cornelius. As he preached to a crowd of Gentiles, the Holy Spirit fell on all who heard his message. Peter was astonished because he heard them speak in tongues just as he had done on the Day of Pentecost. Later, when he was defending himself before the Jewish brethren, Peter recalled how John the Baptist had promised that Jesus would baptize them in the Holy Spirit. He identified the experience of the Gentiles with that baptism (Acts 10:1 — 11:18).

Twenty years later the apostle Paul visited the city of Ephesus and found some disciples there. His first recorded question was, "Did you receive the Holy Spirit when [or after] you believed?" (Acts 19:2). They confessed they had not even heard that there was a Holy Spirit. Paul taught them, baptized them in the name of the Lord Jesus, and laid his hands on them. The Holy Spirit came upon them and they spoke in tongues and prophesied (Acts 19:1-7).

The apostles Peter and Paul, along with James, John, and Jude, were empowered by the Holy Spirit to give us the New Testament Epistles—the Christian's guide to life in the Spirit. Their powerful witness, which they received from the infilling of the Holy Spirit, is still ministering to lives today!

11 Contrast the experience of Peter before and after Pentecost, based on the two charts we have given. Then match the time periods (right) with the descriptions of Peter (left). Write the number of your choice in each blank space.

. . . . **a** Courageous
. . . . **b** An unworthy example
. . . . **c** Unstable as Christ's witness
. . . . **d** Fearful and full of contradictions
. . . . **e** A powerful leader and dynamic preacher
. . . . **f** A cowardly blasphemer
. . . . **g** Impulsive
. . . . **h** A "model" spiritual leader

1) Before Pentecost
2) After Pentecost

TWENTIETH-CENTURY BELIEVERS

Objective 5. *Explain the purpose of the modern-day charismatic movement in relation to Bible prophecy.*

There has always been an outpouring of the Holy Spirit upon the earth ever since the Day of Pentecost, but in the early centuries of the church it was not widespread. The early Christian leaders such as Tertullian (A.D. 160-220), Origen (A.D. 185-254), and Chrysostom (c. A.D. 400), wrote about outpourings of the Spirit with speaking in tongues as on the Day of Pentecost. On through the Medieval Period, the Protestant revivals, and up to the twentieth century, in seasons of special revival there are reports of Holy Spirit outpourings accompanied by speaking in tongues and supernatural ability to witness.

In Acts chapter 2 Peter quoted the prophecy of Joel that the *last day outpouring of the Holy Spirit would precede the great and glorious day of the Lord* (Acts 2:17-21). Peter said the promise of the gift of the Holy Spirit is for "all whom the Lord our God will call" (Acts 2:39). This includes twentieth century Christians! From all the evidence, we appear to be living in the last days. This means that the great and glorious day of the Lord is soon to come, and people of our century are still being called to the Lord.

12 According to Acts 1:8, the purpose for the outpouring of the Holy Spirit on the Day of Pentecost was to give believers what?

....

13 According to Acts 2:38-39, how long was this outpouring to continue?

....

....

The modern-day pentecostal outpouring began in many parts of the world at about the same time. One example of this outpouring occurred in the United States in a Bible college in Topeka, Kansas. The students in Topeka, hungry for a deeper experience in God, saw the experiences of early Christians in the New Testament church as normative; therefore, they studied the book of Acts. In response to their faith and prevailing prayer, the Holy Spirit descended to satisfy their spiritual hunger. On January 1, 1901, the first student was filled with the Spirit, and soon many others experienced the infilling of the Spirit. As they were baptized in the Holy Spirit, they spoke in other languages as the Spirit enabled them. The revival spread to Galena, Kansas, and by 1903 it had extended to Houston, Texas, and throughout Texas. By early 1906 more than 1000 people were filled.

In 1906 a black preacher from Houston, W. J. Seymour, went to California to preach, and revival broke out in the Azusa Street Mission. The meeting lasted for three years, day and night, without a break, and there was a continuous pentecostal outpouring of the Holy Spirit with speaking in other languages and miracles. From there the revival spread all over the United States and Canada.

At the same time, similar spontaneous outpourings of the Holy Spirit were reported in Great Britain, Norway, Denmark, Sweden, France; Germany, and India. The first pentecostal missionary landed in China in October, 1907. Within five or six months, 700 Chinese nationals and missionaries were baptized in the Spirit. By 1909 the pentecostal revival had reached Egypt, Africa, and South America.

Just before the middle of our century, the Holy Spirit began to move in healing power. Evangelists with special gifts of the Holy Spirit conducted great city-wide crusades with thousands in attendance. Miracles of healing took place that had not been in public witness since New Testament times. This move of the Holy Spirit was also a worldwide witness.

In our time we are witnessing a tremendous outpouring of God's Spirit. This move of the Spirit is no longer limited to pentecostal churches as it was at the turn of this century. Instead, we are witnessing the outpouring of God's Spirit on Christians of many different denominations. Since the emphasis is on the baptism in the Holy Spirit and the accompanying *charismata* or gifts, the move has been referred to as *charismatic.* The most significant fact, however, is that the Holy Spirit is bringing the book of Acts experience to people of all denominations, and it is happening all over the world. *This is considered to be a move of the Holy Spirit to prepare the true church of Jesus Christ for His second coming.*

FIRST THE RAIN . . .

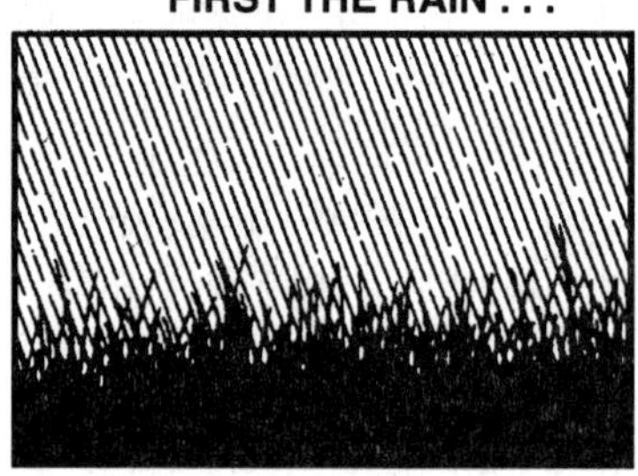

HOLY SPIRIT OUTPOURING

. . . THEN THE HARVEST

SALVATION FOR ALL

A closer analysis of Peter's sermon at Pentecost points out several significant factors. The outpouring of the Spirit, together with the unveiling of supernatural phenomena in heaven above and on earth below—all these are to be accompanied by a universal challenge to heed God's call and be saved (compare Acts 2:17-21 with Matthew 24:3-14). Moreover, when we compare the facts Jesus presents in Matthew 24:14 with Peter's address at Pentecost, we are led to believe that there is a positive correlation between the outpouring of the Spirit and the challenge to evangelize the world. Jesus said, "And this gospel of the kingdom will be preached in the whole world as a testimony to all nations, and then the end will come" (Matthew 24:14).

14 Based upon our evaluation of Matthew 24:3-14 and the foregoing text, choose the best completion to the following statement: Jesus told the disciples that His second coming would take place when

a) the gospel had been preached in the whole world as a testimony to all nations.
b) there were rumors of wars, famines, and earthquakes all over the world.
c) false teachers come proclaiming "I am Christ."

15 Based upon our discussion in this section, what is the purpose of the modern-day outpouring of the Holy Spirit as it relates to Jesus' second coming? (See also Acts 1:8.)

....

....

Are you a recipient of the Holy Spirit outpouring which has swept the earth in these last days? Have you received power to witness where God has placed you? Are you fulfilling your responsibility to give the message to the world? The power of the Holy Spirit which sent the disciples out to reach their world is available to you now. Jesus will come again as soon as the gospel message is preached in the whole world as a testimony to all nations. He has entrusted that message to us. How glorious it is that, with the power of the Holy Spirit in us and upon us, we can work to hasten the coming of our Lord!

self-test

TRUE-FALSE. If the statement is TRUE, write **T** in the blank space. If it is FALSE, write **F**.

. . . . **1** The emphasis in the Old Testament is on the personality of the Holy Spirit rather than on His actions.

. . . . **2** Old Testament believers did not receive the same general outpouring of the Holy Spirit that was experienced by those who lived after Pentecost.

. . . . **3** The Holy Spirit came upon men in the Old Testament to enable them to fulfill a specific function for God.

. . . . **4** Samson and Saul are examples of Old Testament men who enjoyed the presence of the Holy Spirit without interruption.

. . . . **5** The Holy Spirit will depart from a person who is rebellious and disobedient.

. . . . **6** The period of the judges was a time of constant victory for the Israelites as they were led of the Spirit.

. . . . **7** The Old Testament prophets recognized that they could do nothing without the power of the Holy Spirit.

. . . . **8** The main concentration of the Holy Spirit prior to Pentecost was upon the twelve disciples chosen by Jesus.

. . . . **9** A study of one of the disciples before and after Pentecost reveals how the Holy Spirit can change a weak man into a powerful witness.

. . . . **10** The outpouring of the Holy Spirit has continued in the world since the Day of Pentecost.

. . . . **11** Jesus will return as soon as everyone has been filled with the Holy Spirit.

. . . . **12** The present-day outpouring of the Holy Spirit has reached into many denominations throughout the world in what appears to be the preparation of the true church of Jesus Christ for His second coming.

Before you continue your study with Lesson 8, be sure to complete your unit student report for Unit 2 and return the answer sheet to your ICI instructor.

answers to study questions

8 While all the statements reflect the prophets' dependence on the Holy Spirit, a) and c) seem to refer a bit more to personal life than prophetic ministry. I would choose answer b) because it expresses the dependence of all the prophets on the Holy Spirit.

1 a Verse 17.
b He took of the Spirit that was on Moses and put the Spirit on them. (Thus, the same wisdom and power that Moses had by the help of the Spirit was given to them.)
c They all prophesied on this one occasion.

9 c) They were with Jesus most of the time, learning from Him.

2 a To interpret dreams; to become an overseer.
b To lead His people out of Egypt.
c To help Moses meet the needs of the people.
d To lead His people into the Promised Land (Canaan).
e The Spirit's enablement was a relatively long-term experience in each case.

10 Peter.

3 He was from the weakest clan, and he was the least important member of his family.

11 a 2) After Pentecost.
b 1) Before Pentecost.
c 1) Before Pentecost.
d 1) Before Pentecost.
e 2) After Pentecost.
f 1) Before Pentecost.
g 1) Before Pentecost. (Generally, he was far less impulsive after Pentecost)
h 2) After Pentecost.

4 "The Spirit of the Lord came upon him in power."

12 Power to witness about Jesus Christ everywhere on earth.

5 The implication is that the Spirit of the Lord who came upon him (13:25; 14:6, 19; and 15:14) and enabled him had left him (v. 20).

13 The implication is that the promise would be valid as long as the Lord called people to Himself, that is, until the coming of the great and glorious day of the Lord.

6 "Now the Spirit of the Lord had departed from Saul."

14 a) the gospel had been preached in the whole world as a testimony to all nations.

7 Your answer should be similar to this: If the Holy Spirit is grieved by a sinful, rebellious, disobedient life, He may depart even from one who is chosen of God. The Holy Spirit's presence in one's life calls for responsible living and sensitivity to His presence.

15 Your answer. I believe we are living in the last days, and that the twentieth-century outpouring of the Holy Spirit as well as the present charismatic renewal are for the purpose of empowering witnesses so that the gospel will be preached to every tribe and nation. Jesus will come again as soon as the gospel has been preached in the whole world as a testimony to all nations.

UNIT THREE

THE HOLY SPIRIT: A PRACTICAL FRIEND

R. ALLEN

LESSON 8

WORSHIP IN THE SPIRIT

"God is spirit," Jesus said, "and His worshipers must worship in spirit and in truth" (John 4:24). He was speaking to the Samaritan woman at the well in Sychar. Earlier He had told her, "If you knew the gift of God and who it is that asks you for a drink, you would have asked him and he would have given you living water" (John 4:10).

Near the end of His ministry, Jesus shed further light on the meaning of the *living water*. He said, "If any man is thirsty, let him come to me and drink. Whoever believes in me, as the Scripture has said, streams of living water will flow from within him" (John 7:37-38). The apostle John explains that Jesus was referring to the Holy Spirit, whom His followers *would* receive following Jesus' glorification (v. 39). With the Spirit's coming, wellsprings of worship would flow forth from within the believer as a ministry of the Holy Spirit unto God. True worship manifests itself by a holy reverence or fear of God which results in exaltation of the Lord, obedience to His commandments, and a desire to give oneself in dedicated service to the kingdom of God.

Of all God's creation, only mankind has been given the capacity to receive God in the Person of the Holy Spirit and to have fellowship with Him through the Spirit. The Holy Spirit is now preparing a company of redeemed people who will be joined to Christ in perfect communion at the close of this present age and for eternity. Because His Spirit is within us, we desire to worship Him and live for Him until that day comes. What a privilege we have to glorify the One who gave Himself for us that we might have eternal life! He has given us the power to worship Him through the Holy Spirit, the living water that dwells within us! Worship Him, reverence Him, and serve Him!

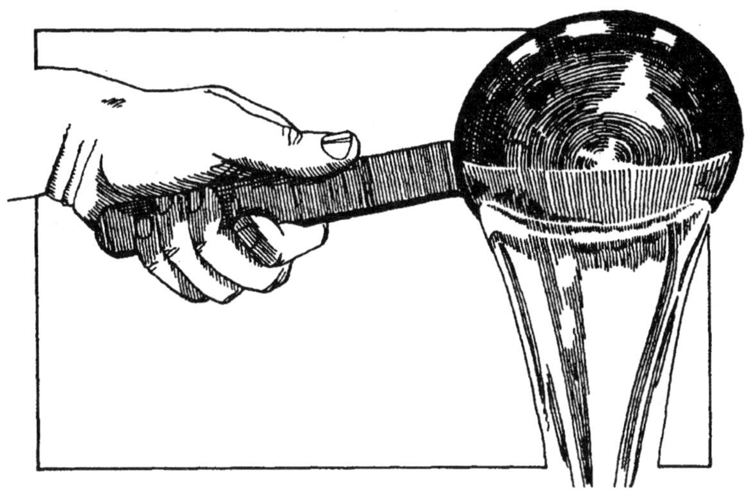

lesson outline

Fearing God
Glorifying God
Serving God
Praying to God

lesson objectives

When you finish this lesson you should be able to:

- Explain the relationship between reverence, or fear of God, and worship in the Spirit.
- Describe ways the Holy Spirit helps us to glorify God.
- Express the importance of service to God as it relates to spiritual worship.
- Develop a personal prayer life and daily walk with God that is worship in spirit and in truth.

learning activities

1 Study the lesson in the manner described in the learning activities for Lesson 1. Read the lesson content, find and read all Scripture texts given, and answer the study questions.

2. Be sure to study the meanings of key words that you do not know.

3. Take the self-test and check your answers.

key words

awe	hallowed
awesomeness	perfecting
contaminates	reverence
edifies	submissive
exaltation	yieldedness

lesson development

FEARING GOD

Objective 1. *Complete sentences from Scriptures which reveal the need for fear or reverence of God.*

Biblical Definition

The wise man said, "The fear of the Lord is the beginning of knowledge" (Proverbs 1:7). Someone else has expanded on this by saying that the fear of the Lord is a reverence that exalts God and that is the beginning of all wisdom. The Holy Spirit helps us to recognize who God is and what He has done. When we see the awesomeness of God, His might and power, we recognize that He is indeed *fearful.*

Fear of God includes the idea of deep reverence, awe, and respect, which leads one to show devotion, honor, and obedience to Him. It is illustrated in the worship experience of Isaiah.

1 Read Isaiah 6:1-8, and answer these questions:

a How did Isaiah describe his vision of the Lord? He saw the Lord as ....

b Would you say that Isaiah's reaction to this vision was one of fear, or lack of fear?

....

c When Isaiah saw the majesty of God, how did he then see himself? ....

d How was he cleansed or purified? ....

e Which of these words describes the response of Isaiah to this vision? *fearful, submissive, unconcerned*

....

The Bible speaks frequently of the fear of God as something necessary and to be desired. This is true not only in the Old Testament where Israel lived under a relatively impersonal theocracy but also in the New Testament where one's relationship with the Lord Jesus Christ is more personal. This is true because God wants us to reverence Him and to give Him the place He deserves in our lives both for what He is and for what He has done. Never should we view our relationship with Him as commonplace nor should we approach Him with irreverent familiarity. He is the Sovereign of the universe; He deserves our unending praise, worship, and respect.

A Growing Reverence

The ministry of the Holy Spirit in the early church brought fear and awe to the hearts of everyone as He worked wonders and miraculous signs among the people (Acts 2:43). As the church grew, it was strengthened and encouraged by the Holy Spirit, and it grew in numbers while living in the *fear of the Lord* (Acts 9:31).

Let's take a closer look at the *fear of the Lord* to see what is included in this concept. Fear of the Lord comes from our conception of the living God. There is a holy fear in us which helps us reverence God's authority, obey His commandments, stand in awe or respect for His majesty and holiness, and turn from evil. (See the following Scriptures: Genesis 22:12; 1 Samuel 12:14, 20-25; Job 28:28; Psalm 111:10.) Those who would *fear* God as they ought may see in Jesus' example that godly fear produced "reverent submission" (Hebrews 5:7). The apostle Paul admonishes believers to let their fear or reverence for God issue forth in conscientious, holy living (2 Corinthians 7:1; Philippians 2:12).

The example of Ananias and Sapphira was a warning to the early church of the necessity to reverence God and show Him the respect that is due Him. Because they lied to the Holy Spirit and their fellow Christians, God's judgment came upon them and they fell down and died (Acts 5:1-11).

2 How did the church react to this? (See Acts 5:5, 11.)

....

The apostle Paul wrote to the Corinthians: "Dear friends, let us purify ourselves from everything that contaminates body and spirit, perfecting holiness out of reverence for God" (2 Corinthians 7:1). He also told the Ephesians to submit to one another out of reverence for Christ (Ephesians 5:21).

The desire to be in God's presence and give Him the honor due Him is completely foreign to the flesh. When Isaiah saw himself in relation to Almighty God, he was filled with fear because of his uncleanliness. But when he was touched by the coal from the altar of God, his fearfulness changed to yieldedness as he worshiped his Creator (Isaiah 6:5-8).

In the same way, our desire to give honor to God is born in our spirit when we are touched by the Holy Spirit, and it develops as we yield ourselves to Him. Those who minister to God around His throne delight to be in His marvelous presence and cry, "Holy, holy, holy" (Isaiah 6:3; Revelation 4:8).

Isaiah speaks of the sevenfold Spirit which would rest upon the Messiah, and which *includes* the fear of the Lord:

> The Spirit of the Lord will rest on him—
> the Spirit of wisdom and of understanding,
> the Spirit of counsel and of power,
> the Spirit of knowledge and of the fear of the Lord—
> and he will delight in the fear of the Lord.
> —Isaiah 11:2-3

The Spirit of the Lord now dwells within us, and we can experience His manifestation of wisdom, understanding, counsel, power, and knowledge. We also learn to reverence and respect God through the help of the Holy Spirit. The intimacy with God that comes through the communion of the Holy Spirit will cause us to respect God more and more as we draw closer and closer to Him.

The Need for Reverence

Paul speaks of the wicked as having no fear of God (Romans 3:18). Yet, Almighty God should be feared above all other powers. Read what the writer to the Hebrews says about this:

> If we deliberately keep on sinning after we have received the knowledge of the truth, no sacrifice for sins is left, but only a fearful expectation of judgment and of raging fire that will consume the enemies of God. Anyone who rejected the law of Moses died without mercy on the testimony of two or three witnesses. How much more severely do you think a man deserves to be punished who has trampled the Son of God under foot . . . and who has insulted the Spirit of grace? . . . It is a dreadful thing to fall into the hands of the living God (Hebrews 10:26-31).

Peter wrote, "Fear God, honor the king" (1 Peter 2:17). This is the way it should be. This does not mean that we live in dread of God, not knowing how He feels about us or what He might do to us. He has been revealed to us by the Holy Spirit as a loving heavenly Father, but a Father that we draw close to with deep honor and respect. Spiritual worship begins with reverence for God, a reverence that will cause us to exalt the Lord and give ourselves in obedience to Him.

3 Find the following Old and New Testament Scriptures, and summarize what each says about the need for fear or reverence of God.

a Exodus 20:20—The fear of God will ....

b Deuteronomy 5:29—The Israelites are exhorted to fear God, so that it might ....

c Job 28:28—The fear of the Lord is ....

d Psalm 19:9—The fear of the Lord is ....

e Psalm 33: 18-19—"The eyes of the Lord are on those who fear him, to ....

f Psalm 85:9—Those who fear the Lord will receive

....

g Psalm 103:11—The Lord .... those who fear Him.

h Proverbs 14:27—The fear of the Lord is...............................

i Malachi 4:2—"For you who revere my name, the sun of righteousness will rise with ....

j Luke 1:50—Those who fear Him will receive His

....

k Philippians 2:12-13—"Work out your salvation with fear and trembling, for it is God ....

l Revelation 11:18—Those who reverence God's name will receive a...

GLORIFYING GOD

In Spirit and in Truth

Objective 2. *Select from a list necessary elements of worshipping God in spirit and in truth.*

Jesus' discourse to the Samaritan woman, which we mentioned at the beginning of this lesson, set the pattern for worship in the church.

This is what He told her:

> Yet a time is coming and has now come when the true worshipers will worship the Father in spirit and truth, for they are the kind of worshipers the Father seeks. God is spirit, and his worshipers must worship in spirit and in truth (John 4:23-24).

Later, Jesus told His disciples that when the Spirit of truth would come, He would guide them into all truth. Then He said, "He will bring glory to me by taking from what is mine and making it known to you. All that belongs to the Father is mine. That is why I said the Spirit will take from what is mine and make it known to you" (John 16:13-15).

Giving glory to God is essential in expressing our worship to Him. The Holy Spirit has come to help us glorify the Lord. He assists us in our worship by revealing the beauty of the Lord to us. We need His help in this because the beauty of the Lord is the beauty of holiness. When we worship the Lord in the beauty of holiness, we praise Him for His moral excellence and purity, for holiness embraces every other attribute of God. As the rays of the sun, combining all the colors of the color spectrum, come together in the sun's shining and harmonize into light, so in His self-manifestation all of God's attributes come together in holiness. He alone is holy (1 Samuel 2:2), utterly separate from evil; therefore, what He does in all His works is right, for His works are the expression of what He is. Having chosen to bring us to Himself through the sacrifice of His Son on the basis of His grace alone, we may approach Him daily with reverent confidence, knowing that He inhabits the praises of His people and is pleased to give them the desires of their hearts. We have no concept of true holiness unless it is revealed to us by the Holy Spirit.

In my early experience as a Christian I was very shy, and the thought of public ministry terrified me. I played my accordion quite well at home alone, but when I tried to perform in even a small gathering of people, I could never finish the song.

Then I was baptized in the Holy Spirit. The night the Holy Spirit came upon me, I felt I could perform before a thousand people, so I agreed to play and sing during the Sunday morning worship service.

When the time came, the boldness that I felt when the Spirit came upon me was gone, and I was shaking. Failure faced me, but I claimed the power of the Holy Spirit and walked to the pulpit. As I began to play the accordion, once again I could feel the Holy Spirit's power upon me and I was able to sing and play. However, as I finished the song I realized something was different—no one seemed to be interested either in my singing ability or my accordion playing. Most of the people in the congregation had their eyes closed and their hands raised in worship to God. The Holy Spirit had been using me, but the Lord was receiving the glory!

As we stated in our last lesson, David is one of the few Old Testament characters upon whom the Spirit of the Lord rested continuously. The psalms of David reflect the Spirit moving upon him, helping him to glorify God. The Psalms are filled with praise and thanksgiving to Almighty God, who is the Provider of all good things. They illustrate how the Spirit can move upon us to lift our voices in praise and exaltation of our Lord and Savior, as we consider His beauty and His sacrifice for us.

4 Which of the following qualities or behaviors are necessary elements of worshipping God in Spirit and in truth?
a) Obedience
b) Praise
c) Boldness
d) Holiness
e) Reverence
f) Holy Spirit's infilling
g) Public ministry

In the Language of the Spirit

Objective 3. *List two ways of worshipping in the language of the Spirit, and give a benefit of each.*

When the Holy Spirit gives believers a revelation of the beauty of holiness, words utterly fail them. Sometimes it is impossible to find words in our human tongues that express acceptable worship. Again the Holy Spirit helps us by giving us the language of the Spirit.

Praying in the Spirit. A dear friend told us how for many years he resisted the language of the Spirit. Yet he greatly desired the fullness of the Holy Spirit and confessed his lack of ability to worship God the way he desired. "Give me the fullness of your Spirit, Lord," he prayed, "but I'd rather not have a language I do not understand." When he received no satisfactory answer, he finally recognized that he must yield himself completely to the Holy Spirit.

After his first experience of worship in the Spirit, he testified that he felt as if a fountain were opened in his spirit that poured out all he had been trying to say to God. For the first time he was satisfied that he had worshiped God in spirit and in truth.

Singing in the Spirit. Singing is an important part of glorifying God. Someone has said, "Music is the language of the soul." We are exhorted to sing "spiritual songs" unto the Lord:

> Speak to one another with psalms, hymns and spiritual songs. Sing and make music in your heart to the Lord, always giving thanks to God the Father for everything, in the name of our Lord Jesus Christ (Ephesians 5:19-20).

> Let the word of Christ dwell in you richly as you teach and admonish one another with all wisdom, and as you sing psalms, hymns and spiritual songs with gratitude in your hearts to God (Colossians 3:16).

Singing psalms and hymns together edifies the whole church and is a witness to the unbeliever (see 1 Corinthians 14). Singing in the Spirit, which is implied by "spiritual songs," helps us to express our innermost feelings of joy, praise, and adoration in the language of the Spirit. Both are important and necessary elements of our worship and both are anointed of the Holy Spirit. The apostle Paul said, "I will pray with my spirit, but I will also pray with my mind; I will sing with my spirit, but I will also sing with my mind" (1 Corinthians 14:15).

5 List two ways of worshipping in the language of the Spirit, and give a benefit of each.

a ....

....

b ....

....

Stanley M. Horton observed that the believers in the early church knew that in their worship they were "quite insufficient in themselves to praise and glorify the Lord. They expected singing in the Spirit, praying in the Spirit, and gifts and ministries of the Spirit . . . . Every day . . . they lived and walked in the Spirit" (Horton, 1976, p. 12).

SERVING GOD

Objective 4. *Identify what given Scriptures reveal to us about the relationship between service to God and spiritual worship.*

Some of the Greek words translated *worship* can also be translated *service.* An example is found in Romans 12:1:

> Therefore, I urge you, brothers, in view of God's mercy, to offer your bodies as living sacrifices, holy and pleasing to God-which is your spiritual worship.

Another translation concludes this verse with these words: ". . . which is your reasonable service" (KJV). Thus, one of the ways the Holy Spirit helps you to minister to God is to enable you to make a total dedication of yourself to God.

The same word is used by Paul in his letter to the Philippians where he says, "we who worship (serve) by the Spirit of God, who glory in Christ Jesus, and who put no confidence in the flesh" (Philippians 3:3).

The fasting and praying Anna did in the temple are called both *serving* and *worshipping* in different translations. When Paul speaks of *serving* the Lord with great humility and tears, the word *serving* could just as well have been translated *worshipping* (Acts 20:19).

It is not so difficult to associate fasting and praying and weeping with worship, but worship is more than that. The writer to the Hebrews said that Jesus offered Himself by the eternal Spirit so that we could be cleansed of our sins and *serve* (worship) the living God (Hebrews 9:14). In other words, the life that we live daily in the Spirit is an act of worshipping God. Everything we say and do can be a means of spiritual worship! That is what the apostle Paul meant when he wrote these words to the Colossians:

> And whatever you do, whether in word or deed, do it all in the name of the Lord Jesus, giving thanks to God the Father through him. Whatever you do, work at it with all your heart, as working for the Lord, not for men . . . . It is the Lord Christ you are serving (Colossians 3:17, 23-24).

SERVING — PRAYING — SINGING

AS UNTO THE LORD!

6 We can learn some things about spiritual worship through service by reading Romans 12 and applying it to our own lives. Complete the following chart by finding the *DO NOTs* in this chapter and state what we are to *DO* instead. This is the first step in Christian service as spiritual worship.

DO NOT . . .	**BUT DO . . .**
a . . . conform any longer to the pattern of this world. (v. 2)	
b . . . think of yourself more highly than you ought. (v. 3)	
c . . . be lacking in zeal (this means *do not be lazy*). (v. 11)	
d . . . be proud or conceited. (v. 16)	
e . . . repay evil for evil. (v. 17)	
f . . . take revenge. (v. 19)	

7 Romans 12 also tells *how* we should serve. Complete the following sentences based on verses 6 through 8 and 20.

a If a man's gift is prophesying, let him ....

b If it is serving, let him ....

c if it is teaching, let him...

d If it is encouraging, let him ....

e If it is contributing to the needs of others, let him

....

f If it is leadership, let him ....

g If it is showing mercy, let him ....

h If your enemy is hungry, ...

i If he is thirsty, ...

Jesus taught His disciples the meaning of *spiritual worship through service* in His parable of the sheep and the goats (Matthew 25:31-46). He has sent us into the world to minister to the needs of others. We are to give them to drink of the living Water that we have received from Him. We are to share the living Bread, the eternal Word, with those who are lost in sin. We are also to minister to their physical needs as though we were doing it unto the Lord. This is spiritual worship put into action!

8 Read Matthew 25:31-46 carefully. Then circle the letter in front of the correct completion to each statement.

The basis for judgment here appears to be the

a) response the hearers have made to the needs they have seen.
b) inability of hearers to assimilate knowledge.

From the Son of Man's response to those who were rewarded we gather that

c) one must work diligently if he is to merit salvation.
d) ministering to human needs is the same as ministering to Him.

Punishment is awarded on the basis of

e) the amount one has done in proportion to what he could have done.
f) failure to respond to the needs of people everywhere as unto Christ.

In this thought-provoking parable, Jesus may be seen as saying:

g) worship, in essence, is dead unless it is accompanied by deeds which demonstrate one's love of God.
h) worship in any form is acceptable with or without accompanying action.

PRAYING TO GOD

Your prayers will be more effective if you follow the New Testament pattern of praying *in the Spirit.* Paul said to "pray in the Spirit on all occasions with all kinds of prayers and requests" (Ephesians 6:18). This is a broad concept that also includes what he calls praying *with the spirit.* Paul says, "If I pray in a tongue, my spirit prays, but my mind is unfruitful [I do not understand what I am praying]. So what shall I do? I will pray with my spirit, but I will also pray with my mind" (1 Corinthians 14:14-15). Both of these can and should be *praying in the Spirit.* You will notice that in this context *praying* includes both *praising* and *thanksgiving* (v. 16), in addition to petition.

Jesus taught us the meaning of spiritual worship in prayer, in what we call *The Lord's Prayer* (Matthew 6:9-13):

> Our Father in heaven, hallowed be your name,
> your kingdom come,
> your will be done on earth as it is in heaven.
> Give us today our daily bread.
> Forgive us our debts, as we also have forgiven our debtors.
> And lead us not into temptation,
> but deliver us from the evil one.
> For yours is the kingdom and the power and the glory forever.
> Amen.

We will look at the beginning phrases of this prayer and see how they relate to what we have said about spiritual worship.

Hallowed Be Your Name—REVERENCE

Objective 5. *Find what given Scriptures say about the name of Jesus, and apply this to your relationship with Him.*

The Lord's Prayer begins with recognition of the sacred respect that should be given to the name of God. When God gave His standard for holy living in the Ten Commandments, He emphasized that His name must be reverenced: "You shall not misuse the name of the Lord your God, for the Lord will not hold anyone guiltless who misuses His name" (Exodus 20:7).

Go out into the street and listen for a while to the conversations of the world. It will help you to understand the importance of reverencing the name of the Lord. Everywhere you turn, you will hear people misusing the sacred name of God the Father and His Son Jesus.

His name is holy. Demons tremble at the sound of the name of Jesus (see Luke 10:17; Acts 16:18). Salvation comes only through the name of Jesus (Acts 4:12). Philippians 2:6-11 explains why we must respect and honor the name of Jesus above every name:

> Who, being in very nature God, did not consider equality with God something to be grasped, but made himself nothing, taking the very nature of a servant, being made in human likeness. And being found in appearance as a man, he humbled himself and became obedient to death—even death on a cross!
>
> *Therefore God exalted him to the highest place and gave him the name that is above every name, that at the name of Jesus every knee should bow, in heaven and on earth and under the earth, and every tongue confess that Jesus Christ is Lord, to the glory of God the Father.*

One congregation of believers was worshipping the Lord recently, and the power of the Holy Spirit came upon them all as they began, one by one, to express the meaning of the name of Jesus. A godly man began by speaking aloud, "*Wonderful* is the name of Jesus. His name is Immanuel, *God with us.*" Another responded, "His name is Counselor, Prince of Peace." And another, "His name is Savior, Baptizer, Healer." On and on it continued, as different persons expressed what His name meant to them. Truly His name is worthy of our devotion! Hallowed is His Name!

9 Find these Scriptures in your Bible, and in your notebook write what each says about the name of Jesus and what this means to you personally. Take time to worship Him for the power of His name.

a) Isaiah 9:6
b) Mark 16:17
c) John 1:12
d) John 14:13-14; 16:24
e) Acts 3:16; James 5:14
f) Acts 4:12; Romans 10:13
g) Revelation 19:16

If you have a Bible concordance, you will be inspired by finding other references to the names of God and the name of Jesus.

Your Kingdom Come—GLORY

Objective 6. *Explain how you can be involved in glorifying God by hastening His kingdom.*

The theme of the preaching of Jesus in the Gospel of Matthew is *the kingdom of Heaven.* He taught that it was "like treasure hidden in a field. When a man found it, he hid it again, and then in his joy went and sold all he had and bought that field" (Matthew 13:44).

Jesus was the man in the parable; the field was the *world;* and the treasure was His *kingdom.* Jesus bought the world with His own precious blood, but He has not yet taken possession of it. The treasure that is hidden from the eyes of the world is the kingdom that the Holy Spirit is now perfecting in the hearts of believers. He is preparing them for rulership when Christ comes back to set up His kingdom.

Paul, under inspiration of the Spirit, says of Christ's coming glory, "No eye has seen, no ear has heard, no mind has conceived what God has prepared for those who love him" (1 Corinthians 2:9). He adds, "But God has revealed it to us by his

Spirit" (v. 10). While our minds may drift on occasion to the blessedness of Christ's presence and the bliss of associating with the redeemed of all ages, God has drawn the curtains aside to give us a preview of the glory that shall be revealed (Revelation 21 and 22). No wonder we yearn for the consummation of God's redemptive program.

10 Did you know that you can have a part in hastening the kingdom of God? Read Matthew 24:14. Then read Matthew 9:37-38 and Luke 10:2. Explain how you can be involved in glorifying God by hastening His kingdom.

What a day that will be, when Jesus establishes His kingdom, and we can sing with the angels around His throne:

> Worthy is the Lamb, who was slain, to receive power and wealth and wisdom and strength and honor and glory and praise! . . . To him who sits on the throne and to the Lamb be praise and honor and glory and power, for ever and ever! (Revelation 5:12-13).

Until that day, let us continue to pray under the anointing of the Spirit, "Your kingdom come"!

Your Will Be Done—SERVICE

Objective 7. *Evaluate your own worship experience to determine whether you are worshipping in spirit and in truth.*

The third thing Jesus told us to pray was, "Your will be done." Who knows the mind and will of God better than the Holy Spirit? In 1 Corinthians 2:9-11 we are told that God reveals His will to us by His Spirit. He can most effectively help us to pray for God's will to be done and then, when the Word is preached, answer our prayer.

The life of Jesus is our example that the greatest way to serve God is to do His will. The passion of Jesus was to do the will of the Father (see Luke 22:42), and the Holy Spirit was always present to help Him (see Luke 4:1, 14, 18-19). You can live as Jesus lived. Your life will also be a blessing to God if you let the same Spirit help you to do God's will.

Romans 8:27 tells how the Holy Spirit will help us: "He who searches our hearts knows the mind of the Spirit, because the Spirit intercedes for the saints in accordance with God's will." Even when we don't know how to pray, the Holy Spirit does, and he will intercede for us for the will of God to be done in our lives.

11 If we pray for the will of God to be done in our lives, we must be ready to obey Him and serve Him. Jesus told the disciples to pray that the Lord would send forth workers into the harvest field (Matthew 9:36-38).

a In answer to their prayers, whom did He send forth?

....

b How can you apply this to your own desire to do God's will?

....

....

12 In this lesson we have talked about *spiritual worship,* or worship in the Spirit. To worship God in spirit and in truth involves obedience, reverence, praise, glorifying His name, commitment to His will, a pure and holy life, and service to His kingdom. Now it is time to evaluate your own worship of God. Is it truly spiritual worship, or is it simply a form of worship without real meaning? The way you can please God best is to worship Him in spirit and in truth. Let the Holy Spirit teach you the true meaning of worship as you yield yourself fully to His direction in your life.

self-test

MULTIPLE CHOICE. Circle the letter in front of the best answer to each question.

1 The living water that Jesus gives, according to John 7:37-39, is
a) financial blessing.
b) the commandments of God.
c) communion with God.
d) the Holy Spirit.

2 Which of these is NOT part of the meaning of *fearing God*?
a) Dread
b) Reverence
c) Exaltation
d) Respect
e) Obedience

3 The example of Isaiah (6:1-6) teaches us that when we are touched by the presence of God we will want to
a) run from the judgment of God.
b) honor God and yield ourselves to Him.
c) follow our own desires.

4 Why is fear of God a necessary part of spiritual worship?
a) It makes us obey Him because we are afraid not to.
b) It causes us to approach God with reverence because we recognize His holiness and that He is worthy of our love and obedience.
c) It is the only way God can fully control us, because we do not have the ability to obey him without fear.

5 Singing in the Spirit is a way of
a) worshipping with the understanding.
b) making known the mind of the Spirit.
c) glorifying God.

6 Another word for *worship* is
a) service.
b) obedience.
c) edification.

7 The principle of service as worship means that
a) everything we do can be a means of spiritual worship.
b) worship can only take place in services within the church.
c) our actions are more important than our spoken worship.

TRUE-FALSE. If the statement is TRUE, write **T** in the blank space. If it is FALSE, write **F**.

.... **8** Romans 12 gives many important instructions about spiritual worship.

.... **9** The parable of the sheep and the goats indicates that helping someone in need is the same as helping Jesus.

.... **10** Praying with the mind is important but is less spiritual than praying with the Spirit.

.... **11** You can determine a person's reverence for God by the way he treats the name of God.

.... **12** The kingdom of God will not come until everyone worships God.

.... **13** In the parable of the treasure hidden in a field, the treasure was the kingdom of God.

.... **14** The only way to know the will of God is to be led by the Spirit of God.

.... **15** It is a good thing to fear God.

.... **16** Worship in spirit and in truth is impossible without obedience.

.... **17** To be acceptable, worship should be expressed in one's own language.

. . . . **18** Singing psalms and hymns is less important than singing in the Spirit.

. . . . **19** Fasting and praying are often associated with spiritual worship.

. . . . **20** The life that we live daily in the Spirit is an act of worship.

answers to study questions

7 a use it in proportion to his faith.
b serve.
c teach.
d encourage.
e give generously.
f govern diligently.
g do it cheerfully.
h feed him.
i give him something to drink.

1 a high and exalted (lifted up).
b Fear.
c As unclean.
d By the coal of fire from the altar of God.
e Submissive.

8 a) response the hearers have made to the needs they have seen.
d) ministering to human needs is the same as ministering to Him.
f) failure to respond to the needs of people everywhere as unto Christ.
g) worship, in essence, is dead unless it is accompanied by deeds.

2 Great fear seized the whole church and all who heard about what had happened to Ananias and Sapphira.

9 a) His name is Wonderful, Counselor, Mighty God, Everlasting Father, Prince of Peace.
b) Demons are cast out in His name.
c) We become children of God through His name.
d) Our prayers are answered and our needs are met when we ask in His name.
e) There is healing in His name.
f) Salvation is given in His name.
g) He is King of Kings and Lord of Lords.

3 These answers are based on the New International Version. If you use another translation, your answers should be similar to these.

a keep me from sinning.
b go well with them and their children forever.
c wisdom.
d pure, enduring forever.
e deliver them from death."
f salvation.
g loves *or* is merciful to
h a fountain of life.
i healing in its wings."
j mercy.
k who works in you."
l reward.

10 Your answer. I would say that I can pray that believers will go out with the gospel into all the world, so that everyone may hear and have the opportunity to accept Christ as Lord and Savior.

4 All of these are necessary elements except c) Boldness, and g) Public ministry.

11 a He sent forth the very disciples who were praying.
b Your answer. I can expect that if I pray for His will to be done on earth, that He will want to use me to accomplish His will. I must be prepared to serve Him.

5 a *Praying in the Spirit*—The apostle says, "I pray with my spirit," which indicates that he prays in an unknown language when he cannot find adequate words to express his worship.
b *Singing in the* Spirit-Helps us through music to express our innermost feelings of joy, praise, and adoration.

12 Your answer.

6 *Note.* For this exercise we have used the New International Version. The words may be different in the translation you use, but the meaning is the same.

a . . . be transformed by the renewing of your mind.
b . . . think of yourself with sober judgment, in accordance with the measure of faith God has given you.
c . . . keep your spiritual fervor, serving the Lord.
d . . . be willing to associate with people of low position.
e . . . what is right in the eyes of everybody.
f . . . leave room for God's wrath (let God handle it).

LESSON 9

SPIRITUAL GIFTS

Do you remember that when Jesus promised His disciples He would send the Holy Spirit to abide in them, He told them, "He will bring glory to me by taking from what is mine and making it known to you" (John 16:14)? In other words, the Holy Spirit would reveal Christ to the world.

One of the ways He does this is to show the world what God can *do*. This He does by the *gifts* of the Spirit. You remember in an earlier lesson we learned that the Father, Son, and Holy Spirit have the attributes of omniscience, omnipotence, and omnipresence. All of these attributes are revealed in the manifestations of the Spirit listed in 1 Corinthians 12:8-10. Supernatural manifestations of the Spirit testify that God is alive and concerned about the needs of people. The gifts of the Spirit were given to the church to *build up the body of Christ.*

You notice that we are using the terms *gifts* and *manifestations* interchangeably. They refer to the same activities of the Holy Spirit. He gives His supernatural gifts as He chooses, and they are manifested through the persons who receive them. The purpose should *always* be to build up the body of believers and to glorify Christ.

In this lesson we will briefly study the gifts of the Spirit and ways they reveal the power of Jesus to His church and, through it, to the world.

lesson outline

Biblical References
Utterance Gifts
Power Gifts
Revelation Gifts

lesson objectives

When you finish this lesson you should he able to:

- List the nine gifts of the Spirit mentioned in 1 Corinthians 12 and write a brief definition of each.
- State the purpose for the gifts of the Spirit.
- Explain who may receive a gift of the Spirit.
- Appreciate the need for the operation of the gifts of the Spirit in the church today and have a desire to receive the gifts.

learning activities

1. Study the lesson in the same manner as you have studied previous lessons. Be sure to read all Scriptures given, and answer all study questions carefully.
2. As background for this lesson, read 1 Corinthians 12 and 14; and Romans 12.
3. Look up the meanings of any key words you do not know.
4. Take the self-test and check your answers.

key words

administrator	edification	reception
discerning	edified	spectacular
discernment	interpretation	supernatural
distinguish	prophecy	

lesson development

BIBLICAL REFERENCES

Objective 1. *List and compare the gifts of the Spirit mentioned in various Scripture passages.*

A study of the book of Acts and the Epistles reveals very clearly that the early church regularly experienced supernatural manifestations of the Holy Spirit. These manifestations were *gifts* to the church corporately for the purpose of edifying the church and bringing glory to Jesus. However, the gifts were manifested by the Holy Spirit through individual believers who yielded themselves completely to the Spirit and allowed Him to work through them.

There are several references in Scripture to spiritual gifts. The most complete discussion is found in I Corinthians 12 and 14. Here the apostle Paul is giving instruction to the church in

Corinth concerning the proper use of the gifts. Nine gifts are mentioned in verses 4 through 11 of 1 Corinthians 12:

> There are different kinds of gifts, but the same Spirit. There are different kinds of service, but the same Lord. There are different kinds of working, but the same God works all of them in all men. Now to each one the manifestation of the Spirit is given for the common good. To one there is given through the Spirit the message of wisdom, to another the message of knowledge by means of the same Spirit, to another faith by the same Spirit, to another gifts of healing by that one Spirit, to another miraculous powers, to another prophecy, to another the ability to distinguish between spirits, to another the ability to speak in different kinds of tongues, and to still another the interpretation of tongues. All these are the work of one and the same Spirit, and he gives them to each one, just as he determines.

The second reference is in verse 28, where eight gifts are mentioned. Some of these have been labeled as *ministry gifts* by Bible scholars:

> And in the church God has appointed first of all apostles, second prophets, third teachers, then workers of miracles, also those having gifts of healing, those able to help others, those with gifts of administration, and those speaking in different kinds of tongues.

It is worth noting that the emphasis in the first list is upon the *gifts,* and in the second list it is upon the *people* who have received the gifts.

1 Three of the gifts in the second list are not mentioned in the first list. What are they?

....

....

Paul continues in verses 29-30 with an explanation of verse 28:

> Are all apostles? Are all prophets? Are all teachers? Do all work miracles? Do all have gifts of healing? Do all speak in tongues? Do all interpret?

Two other references to spiritual gifts should be mentioned. The first is Romans 12:6-8, which we studied briefly in Lesson 8, when we considered the aspect of Christian service as an act of worship.

> We have different gifts, according to the grace given us. If a man's gift is prophesying, let him use it in proportion to his faith. If it is serving, let him serve; if it is teaching, let him teach; if it is encouraging, let him encourage; if it is contributing to the needs of others, let him give generously; if it is leadership, let him govern diligently; if it is showing mercy, let him do it cheerfully.

A fourth reference is given in Ephesians 4:11-13, and includes an explanation of the purpose for the gifts in the church:

> It was he who gave some to be apostles, some to be prophets, some to be evangelists, and some to be pastors and teachers, to prepare God's people for works of service, so that the body of Christ may be built up until we all reach unity in the faith and in the knowledge of the Son of God and become mature, attaining to the whole measure of the fullness of Christ.

Three purposes of the gifts are mentioned here:

1. Building up of the body of Christ
2. Unity in the faith and knowledge of Jesus
3. Christian maturity—Christlikeness

2 In your notebook, make a list of each gift mentioned in these four passages of Scripture, using a separate column for each passage. Record each gift opposite its listing in a previous passage. Add gifts as they appear in later passages. An example is given:

1 Cor. 12:7-11	1 Cor. 12:28-30	Romans 12:6-8	Eph. 4:11
gifts of healing	gifts of healing	not mentioned	not mentioned

Stanley Horton suggests that if these lists are all combined, it is possible to have a total of 18 to 20 gifts (Horton, 1976, p. 210). It is clear that some of them overlap, and some Bible scholars believe that they could be divided into ministry gifts and spiritual gifts. For the purpose of our study, we will use the list of nine spiritual gifts in 1 Corinthians 12:7-11. We have divided them into three groups, as follows:

1. Utterance gifts: Tongues, interpretation of tongues, and prophecy
2. Power gifts: Faith, healings, miracles
3. Revelation gifts: Discerning of spirits, the word of knowledge, the word of wisdom

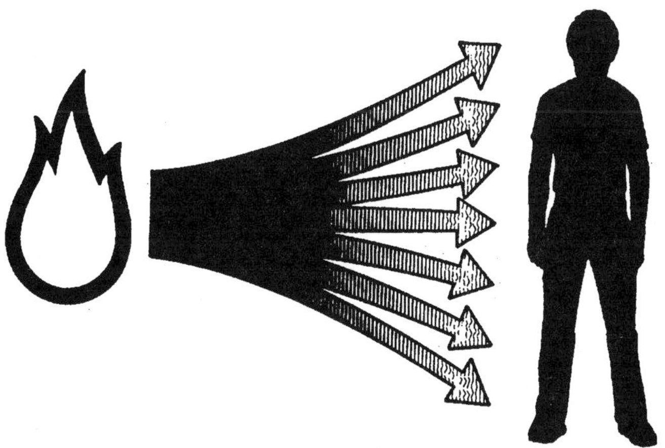

MANY GIFTS BUT ONE SPIRIT

It has been suggested that the utterance gifts emphasize the Holy Spirit's attribute of omnipresence; the power gifts reveal His omnipotence; and the revelation gifts manifest His omniscience. The important thing to remember is that *all* of the spiritual gifts are *manifestations* of the Spirit as He works through the Spirit-filled believer in ministry to the church.

UTTERANCE GIFTS

Objective 2. *Identify true statements concerning the utterance gifts.*

Reception Utterances

The term *utterance* refers to that which is spoken aloud, a vocal expression. In this context it describes speaking in *different kinds of tongues* as the Spirit gives *utterance* or *enablement.* The first physical evidence that one has been baptized in the Holy Spirit can be called the *reception utterance.* It is considered to be the first physical sign that one has received the gift of the Holy Spirit which Jesus promised. The receiving one is conscious of the coming of the Spirit, for he experiences fullness of joy, praise, power, and holy boldness, among other things, as he worships and glorifies God. When the Spirit came at the new birth, He made us aware of our sonship (Romans 8:5-16). He also enabled us to deal with our old self (Ephesians 4:17-32). When He comes later in baptismal fullness, He gives *power to witness* in a dramatic new way. This enduement at Pentecost came to disciples who were already Christ's; this baptism was thus a subsequent experience in the Spirit (compare Acts 8:14-17; 19:1-7).

On the Day of Pentecost the multitude was amazed by the tongue-speaking phenomenon. God-fearing Jews from every nation under heaven *heard the sound* and gathered. They were amazed to hear the wonderful works of God proclaimed in their own languages by Galileans. Since this phenomenon was inexplicable, the apostle Peter gave a Bible-based explanation. The result was a mighty spiritual response. Tongues, in this case, were a supernaturally given sign to unbelievers that the phenomenon they observed was divinely given (1 Corinthians 14:22).

3 Speaking in tongues is a sign to *others* that a person has received the gift of the Holy Spirit. In Acts 10 the account of the apostle Peter's first ministry to Gentiles is recorded. Read verses 44-46. At what point did Peter and the other believers realize that these Gentiles had received the gift of the Holy Spirit? (Choose one answer.)
a) When they were baptized in water
b) When they prayed the prayer of repentance
c) When they began to speak in tongues and praise God
d) When they responded favorably to the ministry of the Word

In most cases, the tongue that is spoken is not understood by the hearers and is never understood by the speaker. There does not need to be an interpretation, because the purpose of the tongues in the reception utterance is to extol the Giver of the gift. While the unknown tongue is also seen as validation of the experience, the transformation of the believer's witness appears to have impressed the nonbelieving crowd more than anything else (Acts 4:13).

Private Utterances

What the Bible says about speaking in different kinds of tongues may be confusing unless you understand the difference between the purpose of public and private utterances of different tongues. The *tongues* manifestation of 1 Corinthians 12:10 is a *public* utterance; it is for the common good (see v. 7). Since this gift is for the edification of the church, it must always be interpreted if the hearers are to be edified.

Private utterances, on the other hand, are for the personal edification of the believer. When you pray or sing in the Spirit in private worship, there is no need for interpretation—it is the act of speaking in tongues itself that edifies the believer (1 Corinthians 14:2, 4). With the help of the Holy Spirit you are able to pray in a way that would otherwise be impossible, because you are uttering mysteries in the Spirit that are directed solely toward God.

One of the greatest blessings of private utterances is the awareness of God's presence when you are ministering to the Lord in the Spirit. You experience the fulfillment of Jesus' promise, "I will not leave you as orphans; I will come to you" (John 14:18).

Private utterances are for you alone, as you worship God. They are always directed to God. They may be exercised as often as you allow the Holy Spirit to manifest Himself through you. Paul was apparently speaking of tongues in private worship when he said, "I thank God that I speak in tongues more than all of you" (1 Corinthians 14:18), for in verse 19 he contrasts his behavior in the church.

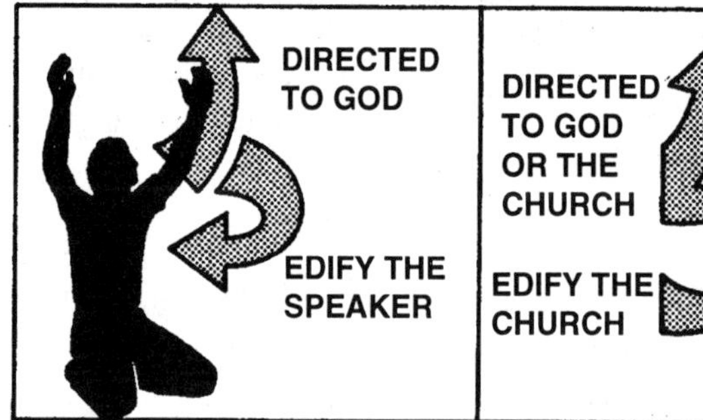

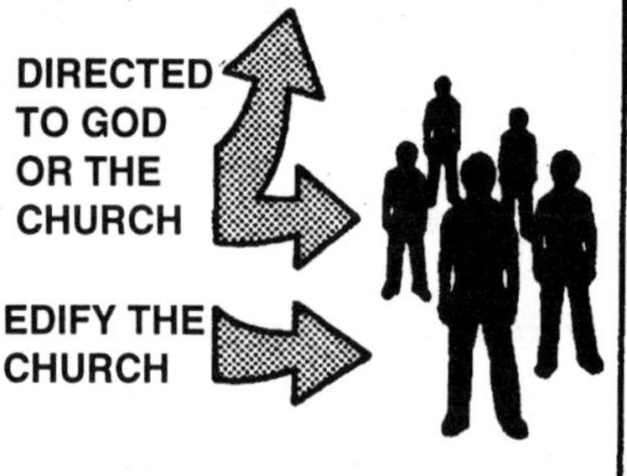

4 (Choose one answer.) An important difference between private utterances and public utterances in tongues is that

a) public utterances edify the church, and private utterances are not intended to edify anyone.
b) public utterances must be interpreted, while private utterances need no interpretation.
c) anyone can have the gift of private utterance, while public utterances are given only to leaders in the church.

Public Utterances

There are three manifestations of the Spirit that are considered public utterances: tongues, interpretation of tongues, and prophecy.

1. *Tongues* spoken in public are always unknown to the speaker, and usually unknown to the hearers. *There must always be an interpretation* (explanation of what was spoken).
2. The *interpretation* is prompted by the Holy Spirit and is given by the interpreter in his own language. The interpreter does not know the language of the utterance in tongues. The interpreter may be the person who gave the utterance in tongues, or it may be someone else.
3. *Prophecy* is a Spirit-prompted public utterance in a language that is known by the hearers.

The purpose of tongues and interpretation is the edification of the church rather than just the personal edification of the speaker. Prophecy, likewise, has as its goal the edification of the church and is the preferred manifestation when strangers are present or when there is no interpreter.

5 Read 1 Corinthians 14:1-5. Why is prophecy greater than tongues unless the tongues are interpreted?

....

....

The objective of prophecy and tongues with interpretation is the same. Through the exercise of these gifts the church can be encouraged, admonished, and inspired as the Holy Spirit speaks to the needs that are apparent to Him. (Romans 8:26-27; 1 Corinthians 2:10-15). Thus, the church is edified. On occasion, the church is directed specifically to implement an earlier commission to win the lost (compare Acts 1:8 with 13:1-3). At other times, He apparently communicates His purpose by forbidding or restraining His servants from certain activities (Acts 16:6-10). Another intent of prophecy is seen clearly in Acts 21:10-1 1, where the Holy Spirit showed Paul things "to come" (John 16:13). The evidence from other Scripture indicates that the apostle Paul received direct communication from the Lord (Acts 23:11) and indirect communication through the medium of an angel (Acts 27:23-24). All of these reveal the Lord's concern for the spiritual life, growth, and development of His church.

There are no recorded examples of tongues and interpretation in the New Testament, but there are several prayers that could be called prophetic utterances (see Luke 1:47-55, 68-79; and 2:29-32). Nevertheless, based on the apostle's extensive treatment of the subject in 1 Corinthians 14, we can conclude that the utterance gifts were abundantly evident in Corinth.

Thus, we can conclude that either prophecies or tongues with *interpretation* are directed by the Spirit toward the church for its edification. Perhaps you have heard a Spirit-filled preacher break forth in prophetic utterance while he was preaching, and you have experienced a special blessing as the church was edified in this way.

The operation of these gifts is to be encouraged, for they bring the presence and blessing of the Holy Spirit into a gathering of believers. However, it is important that the human vessel be yielded to the Holy Spirit so that he will not attract attention to himself, but to God.

The apostle Paul wrote chapter 14 to the Corinthians because he recognized that these supernatural gifts of the Holy Spirit could be abused by believers. If tongues and interpretation or prophecy detract in any way from the moving of the Spirit among believers, or if they are not in accord with Scripture, you will know that they are a work of the flesh, and not of the Spirit.

For a more complete discussion of abuses of spiritual gifts, I recommend that you read Donald Gee's book, *Concerning Spiritual Gifts.*

Paul exhorts us to desire spiritual gifts: "But eagerly desire the greater gifts" (1 Corinthians 12:31). "Follow the way of love and eagerly desire spiritual gifts, especially the gift of prophecy" (1 Corinthians 14:1).

6 Place a circle around the letter preceding each TRUE statement concerning the utterance gifts.

a The term *reception utterance* refers to tongues with interpretation.
b Tongues spoken in private are always directed to God.
c The first physical sign that a person has received the baptism in the Holy Spirit is that he begins to speak in an unknown tongue.
d The baptism in the Holy Spirit brings a blessed sense of the Holy Spirit's presence to the one who receives, and also great joy and holy boldness.
e The most important public utterance is speaking in tongues.
f Tongues with interpretation is of greater importance than prophecy.
g Prophecy is considered one of the greatest gifts by the apostle Paul.
h The purpose of public utterances is the edification of the church.
i When a person speaks in tongues, he never understands the words he is speaking.
j The intent of the operation of utterance gifts is to glorify God and strengthen believers; therefore, these gifts should always agree with Scripture.
k A prophetic utterance may bring an up-to-date word from God that is not supported by Scripture.

POWER GIFTS

The Bible is a book of action. It records the acts of God among men and women. In previous lessons we have learned that the Holy Spirit is the agent who carries out the will of the Father. We have seen the mighty power of the Holy Spirit moving in creation. Then we saw Him moving in miracle-working power in the lives of chosen people in the Old Testament. Next, we saw Him anointing Jesus to do mighty deeds as He ministered among men.

When Jesus left the earth, He said that even greater things would be done by the disciples when the Holy Spirit came to take His place as man's helper (John 14:12). The book of Acts is a record of the Holy Spirit in action in miracle-working power, as Jesus promised.

The Holy Spirit is still moving in the earth today in miracle-working power. He works in the lives of believers who earnestly desire His gifts of power. The purpose of these gifts is to edify the church and glorify God. They are the gifts of *faith, healing,* and *miracles.*

Faith

Objective 3. *Distinguish between the kinds of faith a person can have.*

The gift of faith which the Holy Spirit gives is a *special* faith, and it must not be confused with ordinary human faith, which you demonstrate whenever you sit in a chair and expect it to hold you. Neither is it the saving faith which God imparts to you when you accept Jesus as your Savior, nor is it the *fruit* of faith which grows out of a living relationship with the Holy Spirit, an abiding trust that God will guide you in your daily Christian walk. (We will study the *fruit* of the Spirit in our next lesson.)

Rather, the gift of faith is a special impartation from the Holy Spirit of a faith that can move mountains—an unshakeable confidence that God will provide whatever is needed at the very moment of need!

It is the faith of the three Hebrew men when they were thrown into the fiery furnace (Daniel 3:16-18); of Daniel when he was cast into the lion's den (Daniel 6:21-22); of the apostle Peter, sleeping calmly the night before his head was to be cut off (Acts 12:6).

It is the faith that made it possible for Peter to say to the lame man, "Silver or gold I do not have, but what I have I give you. In the name of Jesus . . . walk" (Acts 3:6). And he walked! In a similar incident we gather additional insight into the nature of these healings. Paul, at Lystra, *perceived* (because of his sensitivity to the Holy Spirit) that the cripple had faith to be healed. Exercising the gift of faith, he called out, "Stand up on your feet!" (Acts 14:8-10). It is this same sensitivity to the Holy Spirit and faith that gave a pentecostal evangelist, Smith Wigglesworth, courage in the early days of this century to walk into a hospital room, lift a dying woman from her bed, stand her up against the wall, and pray in the name of Jesus that she be healed! And she was!

"RISE AND BE HEALED!"

Although the gift of faith is the least spectacular of the gifts of power, it is essential to the gifts of healing and miracles. This special faith is given to certain individuals chosen by the Holy Spirit as He wills, as are all the gifts of the Spirit. Perhaps you have experienced a gift of faith, or have witnessed it in another believer.

7 Give some examples from your own experience of the gift of faith in action.

....

....

8 Match the kind of faith (right) with the description of each (left). Place the number of your choice in each blank space.

. . . . **a** Trust that God will guide you in your daily Christian walk

. . . . **b** Belief that if you get on a bicycle and start pedaling, the bicycle will hold you up and get you where you want to go

. . . . **c** Belief that when you confess your sins and accept Christ, He will save you from eternal judgment

. . . . **d** A special confidence from the Holy Spirit that whatever you ask in the name of Jesus, He will do

1) Saving faith
2) Gift of faith
3) Fruit of faith
4) Ordinary faith

Gifts of Healing

Objective 4. *Recognize examples which give the purpose of healings in the book of Acts, based on given Scriptures.*

Did you notice in verses 9 and 30 in 1 Corinthians 12 that the plural *gifts* of healing is listed? I think the Holy Spirit wants everyone to know that there are sufficient gifts to provide healing for every kind of sickness.

In the early church, these gifts appeared to be more for the purpose of evangelism than for the body of Christ. Healings took place so that the name of Christ might be glorified. (See Acts 3:1-13.) The provision for those in the church as given in James 5:14-15 is that a sick member "should call the elders of the church to pray over him and anoint him with oil in the name of the Lord. And the prayer offered in faith will make the sick person well; the Lord will raise him up."

James exhorts Christians to confess their sins to each other and pray for each other so that they can be healed. Evidently healing for the Christian involves more than just having a gifted evangelist lay hands upon him. There are spiritual needs that should be met by interaction in the body of believers.

9 Read Acts 3:1-13. How did the people apparently react to this healing?

....

10 What purpose for the healing was given by Peter?

....

11 Read Acts 14:8-18. Then circle the letters preceding TRUE statements regarding the healing of the lame man.

a This Scripture implies that both the lame man and the apostle Paul had faith for the healing.
b The people immediately recognized that the healing had come from God.
c Paul and Barnabas refused to accept any personal credit for this healing.
d The purpose for the healing was obviously to give the apostles an opportunity to glorify Christ and tell the good news of the gospel.
e After they explained this, the people stopped worshiping them.

The Spirit-filled church can expect to see gifts of healing from the Holy Spirit, but this does not imply that anyone is given absolute power to deliver from all diseases. The Holy Spirit gives the gifts as *He* wills, and we are exhorted to desire His gifts. The purpose will always be to glorify Christ, and not man. The important thing is to be sensitive to the prompting of the Holy Spirit. If He moves you to exercise a spiritual gift, you should obey Him completely.

Working of Miracles

Objective 5. *Identify miraculous works and determine which is of greatest benefit.*

A miracle has been defined as *God interrupting the ordinary course of nature.* This definition acknowledges that nature operates by a definite set of rules, but that God controls nature and sometimes changes the rules temporarily to work His own purposes.

The working of miracles is probably the most spectacular of all the gifts of the Spirit. It was especially evident in the Old Testament when the Holy Spirit came upon God's chosen ones and they did humanly impossible things.

12 Find these Scriptures. State what miracle took place in each instance and the person God used. Write the answers in your notebook.

a) Exodus 14:21
b) Exodus 17:6-7
c) Joshua 10:12
d) Judges 15:14-15
e) 1 Kings 18:38
f) 2 Kings 4:35

Jesus' earthly ministry was also filled with miracles. They began when He changed water into wine at a wedding (John 2:9) and ended with His bodily ascension into heaven (Acts 1:9). During His ministry Jesus walked on water, fed five thousand people with five loaves of bread and two fish, raised the dead, healed the sick, cast out demons, and did many other miraculous works. The Gospels are filled with His miracles.

Jesus promised that when He went to the Father and sent the Holy Spirit, His disciples could expect the same and even greater miracles to accompany the preaching of the Word. Miracles are not seen as an end in themselves; rather, they attest the validity of the gospel's claims and point to the sovereignty and power of God.

The book of Acts records many miracles of the disciples. In fact, the New Testament record indicates the truth of Jesus' words, "And these signs will accompany those who believe" (Mark 16:17). While many of these miraculous signs and wonders are lumped together in Acts (for example see 5:12-16), careful study reveals a heightened level of miraculous activity. The writer to the Hebrews indicates that the gospel, in the initial years of proclamation, was attended by signs, miracles, and gifts of the Holy Spirit (Hebrews 2:4). These miracles included the raising of the dead (Acts 9:40; 20:10), miraculous release from prison (5:19; 12:6-10), miraculous transport (8:30), prediction of famine (11:28-29), opposition stilled (12:23), judgment of blindness brought on opposition (13:9-12), cripples healed (3:6-10; 14:8-10), demons exorcised (16:16-18), and prison bonds broken (16:25-28). It is thrilling to know that many miracles still attend the proclamation of the gospel today, for God's miracle-working power is still available to us today.

13 Miracles, which are very much in evidence in the New Testament, are intended primarily to (according to our discussion)
a) meet the needs of worthy individuals.
b) demonstrate the power of evangelists, pastors, and teachers to control the lives of these people.
c) verify the claims of the gospel as God sovereignly chooses.
d) satisfy the curiosity of those who seek signs of the supernatural in a church or group.

REVELATION GIFTS

Objective 6. *Match each revelation gift with its definition and with an example.*

The gifts of the Spirit in this group offer special divine insight when it is needed by a Spirit-filled believer. God's knowledge is unlimited, and His understanding of every situation you face is perfect. By the revelation gifts He provides supernatural help when human understanding is inadequate.

We should emphasize that these gifts do not take the place of either natural or spiritual training. Spirit-filled believers need education, and they must faithfully study the Word of God, but there are times when a special revelation of the mind of God is needed. These bits of divine insight are provided by the spiritual gifts called *discerning of spirits,* the *word of knowledge,* and the *word of wisdom.*

Discerning of Spirits

Objective 7. *Identify true statements concerning spirit activity and discerning of spirits.*

The word *discerning* comes from a Greek word meaning "a judging through." The Bible translation used for these lessons calls it "the ability to distinguish between spirits" (1 Corinthians 12:10).

Most of us are not aware of the great amount of spirit activity going on around us at all times. The gift of discerning or distinguishing between spirits allows a brief glimpse into this unseen realm and gives the Spirit-filled believer power to judge which spirit is being used. There are three areas of spirit activity that we need to identify:

1. *The Spirit of God.* God is Spirit, and we need to recognize when He is moving so that we can cooperate with Him. He moves through Spirit-filled believers who are yielded to Him, and sometimes He uses His angels, which are good spirits, to carry out His bidding.

2. *Demon spirits.* The book of Revelation speaks of demon spirits performing miracles in the last days (Revelation 16:14). There is much satanic activity today in the area of the occult and demon worship. The Spirit-filled Christian must be able to recognize the activities of demon spirits, or he might be deceived.

3. *The human spirit.* It is also possible that at times believers are led by their own spirit rather than the Spirit of God. The Holy Spirit gives the ability to distinguish between spirits so that we can recognize whether a manifestation has come from Him, or is a demon spirit, or is of the flesh.

There are several examples of distinguishing between spirits in the New Testament. Jesus knew in advance that Judas would betray Him (John 13:21, 26). He recognized the trickery of Satan during His time of temptation (Luke 4:1-12), and He knew when Satan was the cause of sickness (Luke 4:33-35; John 5:14). Peter recognized that Simon was ruled by an evil spirit (Acts 8:18-23).

The gift of distinguishing between spirits will prevent us from being helpless victims of spiritual deception. This gift can operate only in and through a Spirit-filled believer (1 Corinthians 2:12-15). It is not to be confused with a critical spirit in the natural, which is of the flesh and not of the Spirit.

We gather very helpful insights into the intrusion of error in the early church from the First Epistle of John. Many antichrists, John says, went out from us (2:18-19). They denied both God and His Son (v. 22). Coming to the various bodies of believers these ungodly troublemakers tried to lead believers astray, undoubtedly feigning to give prophetic messages from God to the believers (v. 26, compare Revelation 2:14-16, 20-23; 3:9). John urges believers to test the spirits (4:1) to distinguish between the Spirit of truth and the spirit of falsehood (4:6). He gives certain criteria for judging: 1) Do these people live uprightly, keep the law, and consciously try to avoid sinning? (3:4-10); 2) Do they love their brethren? (3:10); 3) Do they deny Christ's incarnation? (2:22 and 4:2); 4) Do they maintain the sound doctrine proclaimed by the apostles? (2:18-19); 5) Do they share with the needs of their brethren? (3:16-20); 6) Do they listen to the apostles' message? (4:6); 7) Do they obediently follow the Lord's commands? (5:1-3). The Lord of the church has given us criteria by which we can judge spiritual utterances and teaching. It is up to us to be sensitive to the Spirit within as we seek to distinguish between what is good and profitable and what is falsehood.

14 Which of these are TRUE statements concerning spirit activity and distinguishing between spirits?

a Spiritual activity can come only from the Holy Spirit.

b Evil spirits are sometimes able to deceive people and lead them from the truth.

c The gift of distinguishing between spirits makes it possible for a Spirit-filled believer to distinguish between the Spirit of truth and the spirit of falsehood.

d The fleshly human spirit can sometimes copy manifestations of the Spirit.

e Spirit-filled believers must be sensitive to the Holy Spirit and familiar with the criteria for distinguishing between spirits in order to avoid being deceived.

f Anyone can discern what spirit is being manifested.

The Word of Knowledge

Objective 8. *Recognize Scripture examples of the word of knowledge and the word of wisdom.*

We have already learned that the Holy Spirit knows the mind of God. He can reveal God's knowledge to you any time it is needed. It might be a prediction of the future, it might be something that is happening right now in another place that you need to know, or it might be something from the past that you need to recall. You will not be given the gift of knowledge so you will know all things, but only a word of knowledge at the time it is needed.

Have you ever felt the need to stop what you are doing and pray for another person who may be far away from you? Have you learned later that at the moment you prayed, the person was going through a crisis of some kind and needed your prayers? That is an example of the word of knowledge which the Holy Spirit gives to the Spirit-filled believer who is open to His leading.

An example of the gift of knowledge in the Old Testament is found in 2 Kings 6:9-10. The prophet Elisha, who was often called "the man of God," warned the king of Israel not to pass by a certain place because he knew the enemy would be there. Verse 10 says, "Time and again Elisha warned the king, so that he was on his guard in such places."

The Word of Wisdom

The Holy Spirit gives the word of wisdom to let you know what to do in a time of crisis. This is not merely human wisdom based on past experience, but a special wisdom given to meet a special need. It may or may not include the word of knowledge.

Here again, the gift is only a *word* of wisdom. This means that you receive wisdom from the Holy Spirit for a given situation. The word of wisdom is often needful for those in positions of church leadership. A word from the Holy Spirit can bring unity in board meetings and church business sessions. If you are called up before the councils of the world for judgment because of your faith in Christ, it is encouraging to know that the Holy Spirit will be with you and give you the wisdom that is necessary.

Acts 15 records the account of the council at Jerusalem, where the apostles and elders met to consider the question of whether the Gentile believers must be circumcised according to Jewish law. The gift of the word of wisdom is revealed in the letter which the church leaders sent to the Gentile believers, in which they stated: "It seemed good to the Holy Spirit and to us not to burden you with anything beyond the following requirements: . . ." (Acts 15:28).

15 Write a 1) in front of those that indicate a *word of knowledge* and a 2) in front of those that indicate a *word of wisdom.*

.... **a** John 4:7-17—Jesus told a woman about her past life.

.... **b** Acts 5:27-29—Peter gave a solution to a problem.

.... **c** Acts 5:3—Peter knew that Ananias and Sapphira had lied about their possessions.

.... **d** Acts 10:19—The Holy Spirit gave Peter some information that he had no other way of knowing.

.... **e** Acts 28:26—The Holy Spirit gave a message to Isaiah concerning how the Jews would respond to the gospel.

16 State which revelation gift is described in each of the following exercises:

a A special word that lets you know what to do in a time of crisis.

....

b The gift of being able to know whether a spiritual manifestation is of God, of an evil spirit, or of a human spirit.

....

c A revelation from the Holy Spirit of something you need to know at a specific moment.

....

d The gift which caused Paul to recognize that there was an evil spirit in a slave girl (Acts 16:16-18).

....

For a more complete discussion of spiritual gifts and their proper use in the church, I encourage you to study the ICI course in this series entitled *Spiritual Gifts* by Robert L. Brandt. Remember that the purpose for all of the gifts of the Spirit is to edify, or build up, the church—the body of Christ. The Holy Spirit gives the gifts as *He* wills, so that the church will experience spiritual maturity and be strong.

self-test

1 MATCHING. Match the nine gifts from 1 Corinthians 12:7-11 (right) with the definition of each (left). Place the number of your choice in each blank space.

. . . . **a** Gift which reveals whether a manifestation is from the Holy Spirit or another spirit	1) Tongues
. . . . **b** Gift of a special confidence that God will do whatever you ask	2) Interpretation of tongues
. . . . **c** Gift that gives you specific insight into an immediate need and the ability to recall something from the past when you need to know it	3) Prophecy
. . . . **d** Gift of unknown languages	4) Faith
. . . . **e** Gift that interrupts the course of nature	5) Healing
. . . . **f** Gift which provides, in the language of the hearers, an explanation of a message in tongues	6) Miracles
. . . . **g** Gift which brings restoration from disease	7) Discerning of spirits
. . . . **h** Gift of a message from God in the language of the hearers	8) Word of knowledge
. . . . **i** Gift that reveals what to do in a time of crisis	9) Word of wisdom

SHORT ANSWER. Answer the following questions as briefly as possible.

2 Name the three classifications of gifts discussed in this lesson.

....

3 State two important purposes of the gifts of the Spirit.

....

4 Who may receive gifts of the Spirit?

....

....

answers to study questions

9 Apparently they thought Peter and John were able to heal because of their own power or godliness.

1 Apostles, teachers, administrators. (Possibly also *those able to help others.)*

10 To glorify Jesus.

2

1 Cor. 12:7-11	1 Cor. 12:28-30	Romans 12:6-8	Eph. 4:11
wisdom			
knowledge			
faith			
gifts of healing	gifts of healing	not mentioned	not mentioned
miraculous powers	workers of miracles		
prophecy	prophets	prophesying	prophets
distinguishing spirits			
speaking in tongues	speaking in tongues		
interpretation of tongues	interpretation of tongues		
	apostles		apostles
	teachers	teaching	teachers
	helpers	encouraging serving	
	administrators	leadership	pastors
		giving	
		showing mercy	
			evangelists

11 a True.
b False.
c True.
d True.
e False.

3 c) When they began to speak in tongues and praise God.

12 a) The sea was divided—Moses.
b) Water came from the rock—Moses.
c) The sun and moon stood still—Joshua.
d) 1000 Philistines were killed—Samson.
e) The sacrifice was consumed by fire—Elijah.
f) Child raised to life—Elisha.

4 b) public utterances must be interpreted, while private utterances need no interpretation.

13 c) Verify the claims of the gospel as God sovereignly chooses.

5 Tongues alone do not edify anyone except the speaker. Prophecy, and tongues with interpretation, edify the whole church. (Read all of chapter 14 for a fuller understanding of this truth.)

14 **a** False.
b True.
c True.
d True.
e True.
f False.

6 **a** False.
b True.
c True.
d True.
e False.
f False.
g True.
h True.
i True.
j True.
k False.

15 a 1) Word of knowledge.
b 2) Word of wisdom.
c 1) Word of knowledge.
d 1) Word of knowledge.
e 2) Word of wisdom.

7 Your answer.

16 a Word of wisdom.
b Distinguishing between spirits.
c Word of knowledge.
d Distinguishing between spirits.

8 a 3) Fruit of faith.
b 4) Ordinary faith.
c 1) Saving faith.
d 2) Gift of faith.

LESSON 10

SPIRITUAL FRUIT

> But the fruit of the Spirit is love, joy, peace, patience, kindness, goodness, faithfulness, gentleness, and self-control. Against such things there is no law (Galatians 5:22-23).

> Love is patient, love is kind. It does not envy, it does not boast, it is not proud. It is not rude, it is not self-seeking, it is not easily angered, it keeps no record of wrongs. Love does not delight in evil but rejoices with the truth. It always protects, always trusts, always hopes, always perseveres. Love never fails (1 Corinthians 13:4-8).

Jesus ascended nearly 2000 years ago. His followers have held Him up as the example for every true Christian. Some by the power of the Holy Spirit have developed a character so like His that they have reminded people of Him. When soul winners have testified about Him, listeners have said, "Oh, yes, I know him, he's my neighbor." Or, "Yes, I know him, he works beside me at the factory." Even from the deepest jungle has come the reply, "Yes, yes, we know him, he used to visit us and tell us about God." They were talking about people who had allowed the Holy Spirit to produce the nature of Jesus in them.

It is fitting that in this final lesson we consider the *character traits* of a true follower of Jesus, and how these are developed in the believer by the indwelling Holy Spirit. The apostle Paul calls them the *fruit of the Spirit*. They can all be summed up in one word: *love*. They are the attributes of God that are produced in a believer's life by the Holy Spirit. I like to call the fruit of the Spirit expressions of *Christian character*. Examine yourself as you study. Can others see Jesus in you?

lesson outline

Fruit Required
Fruit Reviewed
Fruit Rewarded

lesson objectives

When you finish this lesson you should be able to:

- Explain the meaning of the term *fruit of the Spirit* based on 1 Corinthians 13 and Galatians 5:22-23.
- State why fruit is required in order for speech, service, and sacrifice to be effective.
- Evaluate your Christian character and determine what is needed for Christian maturity.
- Eagerly anticipate the eternal rewards of allowing the Holy Spirit to develop Christlikeness in you.

learning activities

1. Study this lesson in the same way you have studied previous lessons. Find and read all Scriptures given, and answer all study questions. Give special attention to the self-evaluation question, number 10.
2. As background for this lesson, read John 15, 1 Corinthians 13, Galatians 5, and 2 Peter 1:5-11.
3. Take the self-test and check your answers.
4. Review the material you have studied in Unit 3. Then answer the questions for Unit 3 in your Unit Student Report booklet. Follow the directions given in the booklet.

key words

endurance	motivation	purging
martyrdom	persevere	traits

lesson development

FRUIT REQUIRED

Objective 1. *Select true statements which explain why the fruit of the Spirit is needed in a Christian's life.*

As you studied Lesson 9, did you wonder why the apostle Paul wrote about the gifts of the Spirit in chapters 12 and 14 of 1 Corinthians, and interrupted his discussion with chapter 13? You will find the answer to this question by turning to chapter 13. Read the first three verses. Now count all the pronouns you see in those three verses. In the translation I am using, the pronoun "I" appears eight times!

What is Paul trying to tell us? His focus here is definitely on himself as a person. He is saying, "Take away everything I have said and everything I have done, and you have *me*, standing alone. At that moment, *what I am* is far more important than *what I have said* or *what I have done.*

As we saw in Lesson 9, the Holy Spirit comes to help us *do* for God. Mòre important to me as a person, He helps me to *be* what God wants me to *be*. Doing *for* God benefits others most. Being *like* God benefits me most. Both are pleasing to God, but *doing* without *being* is empty and meaningless.

Let's examine more closely what the apostle Paul says about the importance of the fruit of the spirit, or Christian character. In doing this, we will replace the word *love*, which he uses, with the term *Christian character.*

In Speech

Objective 2. *Recognize what it means to have true Christian character to back up your testimony.*

If I speak with the tongues of men and of angels but do not have true Christian character to back up my testimony, it resembles the noisy gongs and clanging cymbals of a heathen temple. My testimony causes people to come to my temple in search of God. But if His nature is not seen in me, they turn away disappointed. My testimony is no better than the gongs and cymbals that call people to the empty temples of the heathen. My true nature does not match my testimony.

The Holy Spirit has come into the temple of your body and wishes to produce the fruit of the Spirit there. Then when you testify of what God can do in the lives of those who receive Him, you will be a living example of your testimony. People will say, "Yes, I know what God is like. He is like you."

1 What does sit mean to have true Christian character to back up your testimony? (Choose one answer.)

a) It means you have a powerful message which will attract people to Christ regardless of how you live.

b) It means that you show the love of Christ at all times, and people are attracted to Christ by what you *are* as well as by what you *say*.

In Service

Objective 3. *Complete statements which summarize the importance of being as well as doing.*

If I have the gift of prophecy, which is the greatest of the utterance gifts—and if I can understand all mysteries and all knowledge, which would be the highest of all the revelation gifts—and if I have mountain-moving faith, which is the greatest of the power gifts—but do not have Christian character, I, myself, am *nothing*.

There is no effort by the apostle Paul here to minimize the gifts. These are gifts of the Holy Spirit. They are the highest manifestations of the mind and power of God that a human being can exercise. They will greatly benefit people in need. Church members will be built up. Supernatural wisdom and knowledge will be shared. Mountains will be moved. God will be praised, and I may be esteemed as a gifted servant of God. *However, if I don't possess the fruit of Christian character, I stand empty before God.*

Jesus affirmed this when He said, "By their fruit you will recognize them" (Matthew 7:16). Then He added, "Many will say to me on that day, 'Lord, Lord, did we not prophesy in your name, and in your name drive out demons and perform many miracles?' Then I will tell them plainly, 'I never knew you. Away from me, you evildoers!'" (Matthew 7:22-23).

Service for God is, as a part of worship, the highest ministry a person can perform. However, when the Christian servant stands before His Master, he will be judged according to what he *is* and rewarded for what he has *done* (Matthew 24:45-51).

There is a reason for this. The Holy Spirit is preparing rulers for Christ's coming kingdom. Since they will reign with Christ, they must be like Him. Positions will be assigned on the basis of Christlikeness, rather than performance alone. Christ will rule with a rod of iron in absolute fairness, righteousness, and love. Therefore, He will look for rulers with pure Christian motivation and Christ-like attitudes. (See Revelation 2:26-27.)

Political offices are sometimes won on the basis of boasted achievements and future promises, rather than godly character. In Christ's kingdom what you *are* will count more than what you have *done*. This is the message of 1 Corinthians 13.

This makes every believer equal. The church member has the same opportunity to be like Jesus as the highest church official. Both possess the same Holy Spirit in the temple of their bodies, and He seeks to produce the fruit of the Spirit in them.

2 Fill in the blanks to complete these statements:

a First Corinthians 13 says that we .... is more important than what we ....

b Those who want to reign with Christ must ....

c Jesus said we would be known by our .... This means that we will show what we are by our ....

In Sacrifice

Objective 4 *Explain the relationship between sacrifice and showing Christian character based on 1 Corinthians 13:3.*

If I give all I possess to the poor, and even if I surrender by body to the flames, yet if I do not possess Christian character, *I gain nothing*.

God loves the poor. Through the writing of the apostle James, He warns that in the last days the rich people will weep and wail because of the way they have oppressed the poor workmen, who have not been given the wages they have earned (James 5:1-4). God is pleased when wealth is shared with those who are in need. Giving to the poor is closer to the manifestation of Christian character than speaking for God, or exercising other gifts, but it does not measure up to the standard of the fruit of the Spirit. What you give will certainly benefit the poor, at least for a while, but your motivation for giving must come from the nature of Christ within you if it is to count for something when you stand before Him.

When Paul speaks of giving his body to the flames (1 Corinthians 13:3) we don't know whether he is referring to martyrdom or to some kind of self-sacrifice for a religious cause that was common in his day. Whatever the case may be, he was in essence saying: "Even if I submit myself to the most painful death possible to show my religious dedication, if I do not possess the fruit of the Spirit, Christian character, *it will profit me nothing*."

3 What is the standard of the fruit of the Spirit?

....

4 When is giving to the poor, or self-sacrifice, acceptable and pleasing to God?

....

5 Why do you suppose the apostle Paul gave the illustration of giving one's body to be burned to emphasize the importance of possessing the fruit of the Spirit?

....

....

6 Draw a circle around the letter preceding TRUE statements which explain why the fruit of the Spirit is necessary in a Christian's life.

a The apostle Paul indicated that what I am is more important than what I say or what I do.
b Speaking in tongues has little or no value when compared with spiritual fruit.
c If I do not have the character of Christ, whatever I do is without meaning.
d People will be attracted to Christ more by what I say than by what I am.
e I can possess all of the gifts of the Spirit and still be *nothing.*
f If I do not want to stand empty before God, I must possess the fruit of the Spirit.
g Jesus said we would recognize His disciples by their gifts.
h Our future position in the kingdom of God will be based on our Christlikeness.

FRUIT REVIEWED

Definition

Objective 5. *Identify words which define what love is or does.*

Christian character is vital, but what is it, and how do I know if I have it? The verses with which we began this lesson give us the answer. In them we find the various aspects of Christian character, of the fruit of the Spirit. As you study them, ask yourself if you possess these attributes of Christ.

7 List the nine fruit of the Spirit given in Galatians 5:22-23.

....

....

True Christian character expresses itself in the fruit of the Spirit, which is summed up in *love*. Out of love come all of the other attributes of God that are developed in the believer by the indwelling Holy Spirit. That is why 1 Corinthians 13:4-8 can be called God's standard of measurement for a true Christian.

The word *love* in Scripture is the translation of the Greek word *agape*. This is a love that flows directly from God: "God has poured out his love into our hearts by the Holy Spirit, whom he has given us" (Romans 5:5). It is a love of such depth that it caused God to give His only Son as a sacrifice for our sins (John 3:16). It is the love of Jesus for us: "This is how we know what love is: Jesus Christ laid down his life for us. And we ought to lay down our lives for our brothers" (1 John 3:16; see also John 15:12-13).

We have paraphrased what one Bible scholar, A.T. Pierson, says about love and the fruit of the Spirit:

> *Joy* is love rejoicing,
> *Peace* is love in trustful rest,
> *Patience* is love on trial,
> *Kindness* is love in society,
> *Goodness* is love in action,
> *Faithfulness* is love in endurance,
> *Gentleness* is love in training,
> *Self-control* is love in discipline.

If you possess this kind of love, which is true Christian character, you will be *patient* (see 1 Corinthians 13:4-7). Whatever you have to endure, you will not lose your temper and say or do things which you will later regret.

You will be *kind* to those who do you harm.

You will *not envy* the positions or possessions of others but you will be content with God's provision for you.

You will *not boast* of your own achievements but will let another's lips speak your praise, and then you will give the glory to God.

You will *not be proud*, because you know that everything you have is a gift from God, and whatever you do is done by His strength.

You will *not be rude*. A true Christian treats everyone with respect regardless of his or her position or status in life.

You will *not be self-seeking*, but rather you will consider God first and others before yourself.

You will *not be sensitive or easily angered*, but you will practice being unoffendable.

You will *not keep a record of wrongs* done to you, but you will always quickly forgive.

You will *not delight in evil* of any kind, but you will remember how Christ was willing to suffer because of it.

You will *rejoice in the truth.*

You will always *protect* that which is right.

You will always *trust* and believe that which is true.

You will always *hope* for that which God has promised.

You will always *persevere* (stand fast), enduring whatever is necessary until faith becomes sight—until that which you hope for becomes reality.

8 Circle the letter preceding definition of what love is or does.

a) Self-controlled	i) Peaceful
b) Self-seeking	j) Envious
c) Self-sacrificing	k) Easily angered
d) Gentle	l) Perseveres
e) Humble	m) Protects truth
f) Rude	n) Proud
g) Patient	o) Hopeful
h) Rejoices at all times	p) Good

Application

Objective 6. *Apply the fruit of the Spirit as it is manifested in the life of Christ to how it is revealed in your life.*

I can hear you say, "Whoever could measure up to a standard like that?" Actually, only one person has. His name is Jesus. You can put His name before every character trait, and it fits perfectly! Jesus asks nothing of us that He did not do Himself, and He did it in the power of the same Holy Spirit who dwells in us.

Christ is our example. It is not possible to imitate or copy Him in our own strength alone. We must allow ourselves to be fashioned in His image by the Holy Spirit. We are partakers of His nature (2 Peter 1:4). The extent to which we partake will determine how close we come to the measure of a perfect person in Christ.

9 Here are some examples of the divine nature of Christ manifested in His life on earth. Match each Scripture passage (left) with the fruit of the Spirit it illustrates (right). Read each Scripture carefully.

.... **a** John 14:27	1) Love
.... **b** Isaiah 53:7	2) Joy
.... **c** Hebrews 4:15	3) Peace
.... **d** 2 Peter 3:9	4) Patience
.... **e** Luke 22:42	5) Kindness
.... **f** 1 John 3:16	6) Goodness
.... **g** Matthew 4:1-11	7) Faithfulness
.... **h** Isaiah 53:8-9	8) Gentleness
.... **i** John 8:3-11	9) Self-control
.... **j** Hebrews 12:2	
.... **k** Acts 10:38	
.... **l** Matthew 18:21-22	

Now let's examine ourselves. Most of us are a little like one of the students who attended our Bible school. Rudy really disliked examinations. He would sigh and groan and seldom answer all of the questions. For one exam he left them all blank, and wrote across the bottom of the paper, "Christ is the answer." But the teacher was equal to the situation. She wrote across the top of his paper: "Christ **100**; Rudy **0**."

That might be amusing, but it has something to say about our final examination day. I know Christ's Christian character score is 100, but I certainly want my score to be better than Rudy's was, don't you?

Paul tells us we will be judged through Christ, by His gospel (Romans 2:16). Perhaps 1 Corinthians 13 will be the very passage which will be used at the judgment seat of Christ as a basis for choosing those who will hold responsible positions in His coming kingdom. This definition of the fruit of the Spirit that Paul has given us could be a self-test that we can study as often as we wish to prepare for our final examination.

All that God requires in Christian character is given in these Scripture passages we have studied as fruit of the Spirit. They are all attributes of God, His character traits. You cannot produce them yourself—you must allow them to grow out of your personal relationship with the Holy Spirit. He will produce these fruit in you.

10 In your notebook, make a chart similar to the example given below, and list all the fruit of the Spirit from Galatians 5:22-23 and 1 Corinthians 13. Mark your progress in developing each of these fruit. Ask the Holy Spirit to produce each fruit in you to the measure of Jesus Christ. How do you measure up?

FRUIT	I can see this fruit in my life:					
	Never 0	Seldom 20	Sometimes 40	Frequently 60	Usually 80	Always 100
Love						
Joy						
Peace, etc.						

FRUIT REWARDED

Objective 7. *State three rewards of fruit-bearing, and give a Scripture to support each.*

Once I was a teenager, but now I am a grandfather. Believe me, there have been many learning experiences between the two. Some were pleasant, and some not so pleasant, but all were necessary.

"Necessary for what?" you may ask. Well, if they were necessary only for this life, by the time I'll be ready to live, life will be over! No, the Holy Spirit is preparing me for something bigger in the near future—something greater than I can even imagine! The fruit of the Spirit, my Christian character, is being developed in me by the Holy Spirit for my place in *eternity*!

Let's look at the last six verses of 1 Corinthians 13 and note some of these eternal benefits.

It Is Timeless

Christian character is the only part of eternity you can possess right now. Everything else comes to pass: "But where there are prophecies, they will cease; where there are tongues, they will be stilled; where there is knowledge, it will pass away" (v. 8).

Prophecies will be needed no more when we see Jesus, so they will end. They will become only memories after they have been fulfilled.

Tongues, both known and unknown, will be silenced when a far superior kind of communication becomes possible through the Spirit. There will be no more language barriers.

The limited knowledge we have will pass away, because prophecy, tongues, and present knowledge are at best only partial revelations of God for this present life. Only the state of our character development as it is at the end of this life will remain. Love never fails—it will remain. Christian character is timeless (1 Corinthians 13:8, 13).

11 (Choose the best answer.) The reason we will not need tongues, prophecy, and limited knowledge in Christ's eternal kingdom is that

a) when we are in His presence we will no longer need these partial revelations, because we will see Him and know Him as He is.
b) we will have no need for communication in His kingdom.
c) when we reign with Him we will have no further need for the power of the Holy Spirit working in us.

It Brings Maturity

We begin our life in the Spirit with the new birth, as we have seen in earlier lessons. Then as we are nourished in the Word under the watchful care of the Holy Spirit, we grow by instruction and experience.

We are all children of God in various stages of spiritual maturity once we have experienced the new birth. The length of time each of us has been a Christian, however, has little to do with the state of our Christian maturity.

The Holy Spirit can produce the fruit of Christian character in our lives only as we cooperate with Him. Some Spirit-filled believers spend many years learning only a few lessons. Tongues, prophecy, And even knowledge are helpful, and they are wonderful gifts of the Holy Spirit, but their presence in our lives is not always an indication of our Christian maturity. The measure of adulthood in God, as we have already seen, depends on how well we have allowed the Holy Spirit to produce the character traits of Jesus in our lives.

12 Read John 15:1-5. These are the words of Jesus. What condition does He give for you to bear fruit?

....

Remaining in Christ involves *union* with Him (vs. 1-2), *purging* or *trimming* (discipline) by the Father (v. 2), and *fruit-bearing* (v. 5). These are the conditions of fruitfulness.

UNION **TRIMMING** **FRUITFULNESS**

13 In 2 Peter 1:5-8 we find the *process* for cultivating the fruit of the Spirit. Complete the chart below by listing the progression which Peter exhorts us to follow in developing Christian maturity. Note where it all ends.

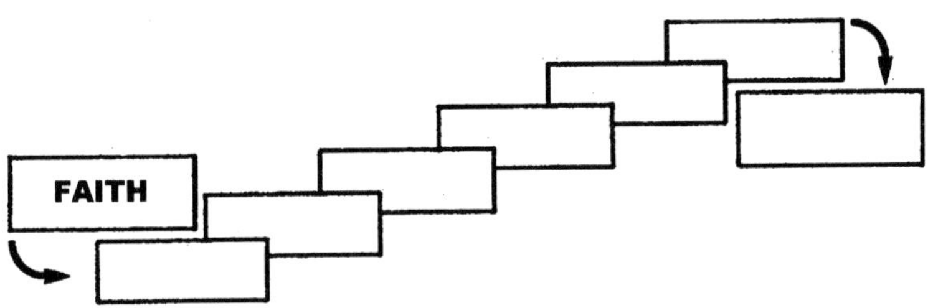

Peter goes on to say: "For if you possess these qualities in increasing measure, they will keep you from being ineffective and unproductive in your knowledge of our Lord Jesus Christ. But if anyone does not have them, he is nearsighted and blind, and has forgotten that he has been cleansed from his past sins" (2 Peter 1:8-9).

It Brings Fullness

When we finally stand before Jesus, our example, we will know what a fully-developed Christian should be like. As the apostle Paul said, "Now we see but a poor reflection: then we shall see face to face: (1 Corinthians 13:12). Now it is like looking in a foggy mirror, but then we shall see ourselves as God sees us. Now we have faith to help us and hope to spur us on, but these are not eternal. Both will become sight when we see Jesus.

The only way to experience the fullness of our reward is to bring forth the fruit of the Spirit in our lives. As Peter reminds us, "If you do these things, you will never fall, and you will receive a rich welcome into the eternal kingdom of our Lord and Savior Jesus Christ" (2 Peter 1:10-11).

14 State three rewards of fruit-bearing, and give a Scripture to support each.

....

....

Self-test

MULTIPLE CHOICE. Circle the letter in front of the best answer to each question.

1 The term *fruit of the Spirit* refers to
a) spiritual gifts.
b) prophecy and sacrifice.
c) Christlikeness.

2 The characteristics of spiritual fruit are developed in a believer by
a) the Holy Spirit.
b) instruction and experience.
c) his own efforts to be like Jesus.

3 The believer's part in developing Christian character is to
a) try to imitate or copy Christ.
b) live according to the law.
c) allow the Holy Spirit to develop the fruit in him.

4 The fruit of the Spirit, or Christian character, can best be summed up by the word
a) *agape* (love).
b) service.
c) faith.
d) witness.

5 Which of these is most important for a Christian?
a) What I say
b) What I am
c) What I do
d) What I feel

6 I can have all of the gifts of the Spirit and still have nothing unless I also have
a) power.
b) tongues.
c) revelation from God.
d) love.

7 In the kingdom of God, the positions of those who reign with Christ will be based on their
a) past performance.
b) desires.
c) Christlikeness.
d) worship experience.

8 Self-control is love in
a) action.
b) discipline.
c) temptation.
d) society.

9 The only thing that will remain in eternity is
a) hope.
b) prophecy.
c) faith.
d) Christian character.

10 The process for cultivating the fruit of the Spirit given in 2 Peter 1:5-8 begins and ends with which two words?
a) Faith—self-control
b) Goodness—godliness
c) Faith—love
d) Love—perseverance

Be sure to review the lessons in this unit. Then complete your unit student report for Unit 3 and return the answer sheet to your ICI instructor.

You have now completed your study of this course. It is our prayer that you have experienced a greater personal relationship with the Holy Spirit as a result of this study. Truly He is a personal, powerful, and practical friend. For further study, we recommend the ICI course in this series, *Abundant Living: A Study of Christian Character,* which is a more expanded study of the fruit of the Spirit. God bless you as you study!

answers to study questions

8 You should have circled all letters *except* b), f), j), k), and n).

1 b) It means you show the love of Christ at all times, and people are attracted to Christ by what you *are* as well as by what you *say*.

9 This is the way I matched them:

a 3) Peace.
b 8) Gentleness.
c 9) Self-control.
d 4) Patience.
e 7) Faithfulness.
f 1) Love.
g 9) Self-control.
h 6) Goodness.
i 5) Kindness.
j 2) Joy.
k 6) Goodness.
l 4) Patience.

2 a are, do.
b be like Him.
c fruit, Christian character.

10 Your answer.

3 Love, or Christian character.

11 a) when we are in His presence we will no longer need these partial revelations.

4 When it is done with the kind of love that Christ has for us.

12 In order to bear fruit, you must remain in Him.

5 Your answer. I would say that he wanted to impress upon us that showing love as Christ shows it is the only thing that will count in eternity. He used self-sacrifice as the most extreme act a person could *do*, to show that what we *are* is more important.

13

BROTHERLY KINDNESS

GODLINESS

PERSEVERANCE **LOVE**

FAITH SELF-CONTROL

KNOWLEDGE

GOODNESS

6 a True.
b False.
c True.
d False.
e True.
f True.
g False.
h True.

14 Spiritual fruit, or love , is *timeless*: 1 Corinthians 13:8, 13. It brings *Christian maturity*, or Christlikeness: 2 Peter 1:8. It brings *fullness*: 2 Peter 1:10-11.

7 Love, joy, peace, patience, kindness, goodness, faithfulness, gentleness, self-control.

BIBLIOGRAPHY

Bickersteth, Edward Henry. *The Holy Spirit: His Person and Work.* Grand Rapids, Michigan: Kregel Publications, 1973.

Biederwolf, William E. *A. Help to the Study of the Holy Spirit.* Grand Rapids, Michigan: Baker Book House, 1974.

Gee, Donald. *Concerning Spiritual Gifts.* Springfield, Missouri: Gospel Publishing House, 1947.

Horton, Stanley M. *What the Bible Says About the Holy Spirit.* Springfield, Missouri: Gospel Publishing House, 1976.

____________. *The Holy Spirit: A Study Guide.* Brussels, Belgium: International Correspondence Institute, 1979.

Thiessen, Henry C. *Lectures in Systematic Theology.* Revised by Vernon D. Doerksen. Grand Rapids, Michigan: William B. Eerdmans Publishing Company, 1979.

GLOSSARY

The right-hand column lists the lesson in this independent-study textbook in which the word is first used.

		Lesson
Abba	— Aramaic word for *Father*	6
acclamation	— a strong expression of approval, praise, or assent	2
accomplishments	— things achieved, completed	7
administrative	— of or relating to the performance of executive or leadership duties	1
administrator	— a person who carries out executive (leadership) duties	9
anointing	— in the Old Testament, the pouring of oil upon the head to designate someone for a special purpose; in the New Testament, the Holy Spirit coming upon someone to give enablement for a special purpose	5
anoints	— enables; empowers for a specific purpose	3
astronomer	— one who is skilled in the study of heavenly bodies	4
astronomy	— the science of the celestial (heavenly) bodies (such as sun, moon, stars)	4

attributes	— the qualities or characteristics of a person or thing	2
awe	— a profound and reverent fear; reverent wonder	8
awesomeness	— the capacity of inspiring reverence, fear, and wonder	8
benediction	— a short blessing which concludes a prayer	2
blasphemy	— the act of insulting or showing lack of reverence for God	1
canon	— an authoritative list of books accepted as Holy Scripture	3
celestial	— of, or relating to, or suggesting heaven	4
charismatic	— a name given sometimes to modern-day pentecostals; related to the pentecostal experience of the baptism in the Holy Spirit with speaking in unknown tongues	7
commissioning	— giving authority to act for, in behalf of, or in place of another	1
concentration	— emphasis; center of efforts or attention	7
confirms	— gives approval to; agrees with	7
conform	— to bring into harmony or agreement; to be similar	6
contaminates	— soils, stains, or infects by contact or association	8

contend	— to struggle for; to strive against	1
contradictions	— actions of a person that are the opposite of their other actions	7
conviction	— the state of being convinced of error; a strong belief	3
counselor	— one who gives advice or help	1
deity	— supreme being; God	2
descent	— the act of moving from a higher level to a lower	5
designation	— the act of indicating or identifying	1
discerning	— separating or distinguishing between	9
discernment	— sharp insight; skill in distinguishing between	9
distinguish	— to mark as separate or different	9
edification	— the act or process of building up, instructing, or improving spiritually	9
edified	— enlightened; instructed or improved spiritually	9
edifies	— enlightens; instructs or improves spiritually	8
elders	— ones who have authority by virtue of age or experience	1
emotional	— capable of expressing feelings	1
empowering	— enabling; giving power	7

enduement	— provision; endowment	7
endurance	— the ability to remain firm; ability to undergo hardship	10
enlightens	— instructs; illuminates; furnishes knowledge to; makes clear	3
exaltation	— an act of raising high in praise and adoration	8
finite	— having a limited nature or existence	4
fulfillment	— satisfaction; completion	7
glorified	— given praise, honor, or distinction	6
grieve	— to make sad	1
hallowed	— sacred, consecrated	8
heirs	— ones who are entitled to receive the property or gifts of another	6
hover	— to remain suspended over a place or object; to brood over; to move to and fro near a place	4
illuminates	— makes clear; enlightens	1
illumination	— the state of being made clear; enlightenment	5
impartation	— a gift or grant from one's store of abundance	4
impulsive	— likely to act without thinking it through	7
Incarnate	— having human form; Jesus is the Incarnate Son of God, who took a human form	2

indwelling	— existing within	7
infallible	— without error; perfect	5
infilling	— a filling within	7
inheritance	— something that is received as the right of an heir	3
inspiration	— the divine power of the Holy Spirit upon a person's intellect or emotions to express the mind of God	5
inspire	— a work of the Holy Spirit to express the mind of God upon a person's intellect or emotions	3
intercedes	— acts between two parties to bring about agreement	1
intercessor	— one who prays, petitions, or entreats in favor of another	3
interpretation	— the act or result of explaining the meaning of something	9
interpreter	— one who explains the meaning of something	3
intimate	— marked by a very close association; of a very personal or private nature	1

---

manifestation	— that which is made evident by showing or displaying	2
manifested	— made evident or certain by showing or displaying	1
marred	— spoiled; damaged	1

martyrdom	— the suffering of death on account of one's religious faith or another cause	10
mediator	— one who stands between two parties to bring accord	3
misconduct	— intentional wrongdoing	1
motivation	— a force such as a need or desire that causes a person to act	10
neuter	— being neither masculine nor feminine in gender	1
nurture	— bring up; care for; train	2
omnipotent	— having unlimited power	2
omnipresent	— being everywhere present	2
omniscient	— knowing all things	2
ordeal	— a severe trial or experience	5
oriented	— acquainted with a situation or environment	1
Paraclete	— refers to the Holy Spirit as Comforter	3
partakers	— those who share in something	6
Pentateuch	— the first five books of the Old Testament	7
pentecostal	— relating to the experience of the baptism in the Holy Spirit; one who has had the experience	7
perfecting	— act of making perfect	8
perish	— to die	6

persevere	— to stand fast for what you believe; to persist in the face of opposition	10
preexistence	— speaks of having being before the beginning of time	4
presumptuous	— overstepping the boundaries given; taking liberties without authority	7
prophecy	— an inspired utterance	9
prophesying	— speaking under divine inspiration	6
purging	— removing; getting rid of	10
purity	— the quality of being spotless, without sin	2

---

reception	— the act of welcoming or receiving	9
receptive	— able or inclined to receive	7
recipient	— one who receives	7
redemption	— the act of releasing from blame or debt; the act of winning back	3
regeneration	— the process of becoming renewed or reborn	3
repentance	— the act or process of changing one's mind; being sorry and turning from sin	6
repentant	— expressing or showing sorrow for sin and a desire to change	3
resistance	— opposition	6
revelation	— the making known of something previously not known	3

reverence	— honor or respect; profound, adoring awe	8
righteousness	— justice; that which is according to what is right	3
sanctification	— the state of being set apart unto God; holiness	6
sanctify	— to set apart unto God; to make holy	6
seal	— something that confirms or makes secure	3
sensitive	— capable of feeling	1
solar system	— the sun with the group of celestial bodies that are held by its attraction and revolve around it	4
sovereign	— possessed of supreme power	2
spectacular	— having an eye-catching or dramatic display	9
spokesman	— one who speaks as the representative of another	3
spontaneous	— developing without apparent outside influence; unplanned; automatic	7
submissive	— yielding to others	8
sufficiency	— adequacy; ability to meet needs	2
supernatural	— beyond the natural or normal; of or relating to God	9
sustaining	— keeping up; supporting	4

traits	— qualities or characteristics	10
transformed	— changed completely	2
transgressions	— sins; violations	6
Trinity	— the three Persons of the Godhead: Father, Son, and Holy Spirit	2
Triune	— three-in-one; relating to the Trinity	2
unblemished	— without defects or flaws	5
universe	— the heavens and the earth and all that is contained within them	4
utterance	— something spoken; an oral or written statement	3
vegetation	— plant life	4
yieldedness	— submission; giving of oneself completely	8

ANSWERS TO SELF-TESTS

Lesson 1

1 False.

2 True.

3 True.

4 True.

5 False.

6 True.

7 False.

8 False.

9 True.

10 problems

11 desires

12 experience

13 relationship

14 maturity

15 complete

16 Ability to feel, know, and choose.

17 Because He is a Person, He can love me, and I can return His love. He can also love others through me.

18 Any of these: He can be lied to, resisted, insulted, blasphemed, sinned against.

Lesson 2

1 False.

2 True.

3 True.

4 False.

5 False.

6 True.

7 True.

8 False.

9 True.

10 True.

11 False.

12 True.

13 You should have circled all letters except b), d), and j).

14 By the association in each of God the Father, God the Son, and God the Holy Spirit.

15 Because He possesses the attributes of divinity, He gives me spiritual life, power, holiness, and companionship.

Lesson 3

1 c) Creator.

2 d) One called alongside to help.

3 b) regeneration.

4 a) spiritual birth.

5 c) Satan.

6 a) He disciplines us.

7 d) Perfection.

8 c) Intercessor.

9 a) Guide.

10 Any two: Bring the things of Christ to our remembrance, testify about Christ, guide us into all truth, glorify Christ, give us a knowledge of future events in God's plan.

11 Jesus, Holy Spirit, believer.

Lesson 4

1 b) little about individual involvement, but emphasizes the plurality of the one eternal God and that He is the Creator of all things.

2 c) Man's need for redemption.

3 a) before the beginning of time.

4 b) the preexistence of the Trinity in relation to the time of Creation.

5 a) the Father, the Son, and the Holy Spirit.

6 c) move in power to carry out the divine decree.

7 c) Imparting the breath of life which made man a spiritual being.

8 a) sustaining all that was created.

9 b) display His glory and receive glory.

10 b) Worship and obey Him.

11 b) Man was formed by God from dust.

12 b) The people were not ready to receive the revelation of a Triune God.

Lesson 5

1 c) acting upon what we heard.

2 b) changed as it was passed on.

3 d) without error.

4 b) revelation.

5 a) Scripture in its fullest extent was inspired by the Holy Spirit.

6 c) understand the meaning of Scriptures.

7 a) The Bible's unity.

8 c) the guidance of the Holy Spirit.

9 c) is still doing today what it says it will do in the lives of men.

10 b) His baptism.

11 e) answers a) and c).

12 a) ruled by the Spirit.

Lesson 6

1 a) This is a work of the Holy Spirit . . .

2 b) Although it is the Holy Spirit who convicts a sinner...

3 b) Repentance involves a change . .

4 b) I no longer live according to the sinful nature . . .

5 a) When the Holy Spirit takes up residence I receive personal benefits . . .

6 a) As I yield myself to the Holy Spirit's control, He enables me to separate myself from sin and unto God.

7 b) When the Holy Spirit gives me new birth . . .

Lesson 7

1 False.

2 True.

3 True.

4 False.

5 True.

6 False.

7 True.

8 False.

9 True.

10 True.

11 False.

12 True.

16 True.

17 False.

18 False.

19 True.

20 True.

Lesson 8

1 d) the Holy Spirit.

2 a) Dread.

3 b) honor God and yield ourselves to Him.

4 b) it causes us to approach God with reverence because we recognize His holiness.

5 c) glorifying God.

6 a) service.

7 a) everything we do can be a means of spiritual worship.

8 True.

9 True.

10 False.

11 True.

12 False.

13 True.

14 True.

15 True.

Lesson 9

1 **a** 7) Discerning of spirits.
b 4) Faith.
c 8) Word of knowledge.
d 1) Tongues.
e 6) Miracles.
f 2) Interpretation of tongues.
g 5) Healing.
h 3) Prophecy.
i 9) Word of wisdom.

2 Utterance gifts, power gifts, and revelation gifts.

3 Edify the church, glorify Christ.

4 Any Spirit-filled believer. (But they are given as the Holy Spirit chooses. We are encouraged to desire the gifts of the Spirit. This suggests that those who earnestly desire the gifts are the ones whom the Holy Spirit chooses.)

Lesson 10

1 c) Christlikeness.

2 a) the Holy Spirit.

3 c) allow the Holy Spirit to develop the fruit in him.

4 a) *agape* (love).

5 b) What I am.

6 d) love.

7 c) Christlikeness.

8 b) discipline.

9 d) Christian character.

10 c) Faith—love.

CS3331

Counselor, Teacher, and Guide

UNIT STUDENT REPORTS
AND
ANSWER SHEETS

DIRECTIONS

When you have completed your study of each unit, fill out the unit student report answer sheet for that unit. The following are directions how to indicate your answer to each question. There are two kinds of questions: TRUE-FALSE and MULTIPLE-CHOICE.

TRUE-FALSE QUESTION EXAMPLE

The following statement is either true or false. If the statement is

TRUE, blacken space A.
FALSE, blacken space B.

1 The Bible is God's message for us.

The above statement, *The Bible is God's message for us,* is TRUE, so you would blacken space A like this:

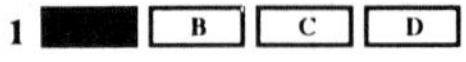

MULTIPLE CHOICE QUESTION EXAMPLE

There is one best answer for the following question. Blacken the space for the answer you have chosen.

2 To be born again means to
a) be young in age.
b) accept Jesus as Savior.
c) start a new year.
d) find a different church.

The correct answer is b) *accept Jesus as Savior,* so you would blacken space B like this:

STUDENT REPORT FOR UNIT ONE

Answer all questions on Unit Student Report Answer Sheet 1. See the examples on the **DIRECTIONS** *page which show you how to mark your answers.*

PART 1—TRUE-FALSE QUESTIONS

The following statements are either true or false. If the statement is
TRUE, blacken space a space A.
FALSE, blacken space B.

1 I have carefully read all of the lessons in Unit One.

2 The Holy Spirit's existence is eternal.

3 The Holy Spirit is the Third Person of the Trinity, but with less power than God the Father and God the Son.

4 The Holy Spirit possesses some but not all of the attributes of God.

5 The Holy Spirit convinces the world of sin, righteousness, and judgment.

6 The term Paraclete means "righteous judge."

7 If we know the Holy Spirit as a Person, spiritual experiences are more important than our relationship with Him.

8 The qualities, offices, and designations of the Holy Spirit all indicate that He is a Person.

PART 2—MULTIPLE-CHOICE QUESTIONS

There is one best answer for each of the following questions. Blacken the space on your answer sheet for the answer you have chosen.

9 The baptismal formula and the apostolic benediction are evidence that the Holy Spirit
a) has personality.
b) is on a lower level than the Father and the Son.
c) is divine.

10 Which of these is NOT an attribute of deity?
a) Eternal
b) Omnipotent
c) Changeable
d) Omnipresent

11 *Omniscient* means
a) all-powerful.
b) holy.
c) all-seeing.
d) all-knowing.

12 Which of these is NOT included in the divine sufficiency of the Holy Spirit?
a) He bestows holiness.
b) He makes our choices.
c) He gives power.
d) He imparts spiritual life.

13 If you are experience oriented you will see the baptism in the Holy Spirit as
a) an end in itself.
b) the beginning of a wonderful relationship.
c) involving a divine Person.
d) a door to spiritual maturity.

14 The use of the pronouns *he* and *him* in Scripture references to the Holy Spirit indicate His
a) personality.
b) deity.
c) sovereignty.

15 As an emotional being, the Holy spirit has
a) knowledge.
b) will.
c) desires.

16 In His office of Comforter the Holy Spirit is sent alongside to
a) teach.
b) help.
c) administer.
d) judge.

17 The proof the Holy Spirit has to convince the world of the righteousness of Jesus is that Jesus
a) died on the cross.
b) taught on righteousness.
c) returned to His Father in heaven.
d) performed miracles.

18 The Holy Spirit convinces the world of judgment by reminding them of the judgment of
a) fallen man.
b) God's chosen people.
c) spirit beings.
d) Satan.

19 As our Counselor the Holy Spirit
a) provides instruction, illumination, and direction for our lives.
b) talks to God about us.
c) talks to us about God.
d) helps us with our problems, both physical and spiritual.

20 In His function as our intercessor, the Holy Spirit
a) offers us advice about decisions we need to make.
b) helps us present our needs to God.
c) comforts us when we are sad.

END OF REQUIREMENTS FOR UNIT ONE. Follow the remaining instructions on your answer sheet and return it to your ICI Instructor or office in your area, then begin your study of Unit Two.

STUDENT REPORT FOR UNIT TWO

Answer all questions on Answer Sheet for Unit Two. See the examples on the **DIRECTIONS** *page which show you how to mark your answers.*

PART 1—TRUE-FALSE QUESTIONS

The following statements are either true or false. If the statement is

TRUE, blacken space A.
FALSE, blacken space B.

1 I have carefully read all of the lessons in Unit Two.

2 The Holy Spirit spoke the word and the waters divided at Creation.

3 When God created man, He expected that man would be obedient to Him.

4 A written communication is better than an oral one.

5 Although about 40 men wrote the Bible, it has complete unity.

6 The conviction of the Holy Spirit always brings repentance.

7 It is the Holy Spirit who imparts spiritual life.

8 The main purpose of the outpouring of the Holy Spirit is to provide supernatural manifestations in the church.

PART 2—MULTIPLE-CHOICE QUESTIONS

There is one best answer for each of the following questions. Blacken the space on your answer sheet for the answer you have chosen.

9 The doctrine of the Trinity was not known at the time of Moses because God's self-revelation

a) is progressive.
b) is known only by a Spirit-filled believer.
c) took place on the Day of Pentecost.

10 Creation was an activity of
a) God the Father.
b) God the Father and the Holy Spirit.
c) all three Persons in the Trinity.
d) God the Father and His Son.

11 At Creation man received life when God
a) formed him out of dust.
b) breathed into him.
c) spoke the word.
d) gave him a companion.

12 When the power of the Holy Spirit moves upon a man's intellect to
express the mind of God, this is called
a) revelation.
b) illumination.
c) doctrine.
d) inspiration.

13 Plenary inspiration means that
a) Scripture in its fullest extent is inspired by the Holy Spirit.
b) some Scriptures are inspired.
c) the Holy Spirit inspires those who read the Scriptures.
d) the doctrines are inspired, but the recording of history is not inspired.

14 The role of the Holy Spirit in the life and ministry of Jesus included preparing, anointing, and
a) tempting Him through Satan.
b) suffering for Him.
c) crowning the living Word.
d) disciplining by the Word.

15 Being set apart unto God and transformed progressively into the image of Christ is a work of the Holy Spirit called
a) regeneration.
b) sanctification.
c) adoption.
d) repentance.

16 As the Spirit of adoption the Holy Spirit gives new birth and
a) makes me sinless.
b) gives me status as an adult in God's family.
c) produces the fruit of the Spirit.
d) changes my way of living.

17 When the apostle Paul said that we are God's temple, he meant that if we are believers
a) most of our time is spent in worship.
b) we are free from the law of sin and death.
c) we should be involved in the work of the church.
d) the Holy Spirit dwells within us.

18 In the Old Testament, the Holy Spirit usually came upon chosen men so that they could
a) have revelations from God.
b) be victorious over enemies.
c) perform a specific service.
d) experience God's presence.

19 The experiences of both Old and New Testament men of God confirm that the Holy Spirit
a) does not try to change a person's behavior.
b) transforms weakness into power.
c) chooses strong men to do His work.
d) functions best through men with great leadership ability.

20 Which statement best describes what followed the outpouring of the Holy Spirit which began on the Day of Pentecost?

a) Since then the Holy Spirit's ministry has been apparent in the church.
b) That special outpouring ended with the early church.
c) All Christians have experienced the outpouring of the Holy Spirit.

END OF REQUIREMENTS FOR UNIT TWO. Follow the remaining instructions on your answer sheet and return it to your ICI instructor or office in your area, then begin your study of Unit Three.

STUDENT REPORT FOR UNIT THREE

Answer all questions on Answer Sheet for Unit Three. See the examples on the **DIRECTIONS** *page which show you how to mark your answers.*

PART 1—TRUE-FALSE QUESTIONS

The following statements are either true or false. If the statement is

TRUE, blacken space A.
FALSE, blacken space B.

1 I have carefully read all of the lessons in Unit Three.

2 The Bible speaks of the fear of God as unnecessary.

3 The purpose of worship is to give glory to God.

4 The purpose of spiritual gifts is to show believers who is the most spiritual among them.

5 Spiritual gifts are limited to the nine gifts listed in 1 Corinthians 12.

6 What I am is more important than what I say or do.

7 Possessing the gifts of the Spirit is more important than possessing the fruit of the Spirit.

8 The standard of the fruit of the Spirit is love.

PART 2—MULTIPLE-CHOICE QUESTIONS

There is one best answer for each of the following questions. Blacken the space on your answer sheet for the answer you have chosen.

9 Which of these words best defines the term "fear of the Lord"?
a) Concern
b) Majesty
c) Holiness
d) Reverence

10 Which of these is NOT something produced by the fear of the Lord? The fear of the Lord
a) keeps me from sinning.
b) brings salvation.
c) provides healing.
d) leads to death.

11 Praying and singing in the Spirit helps us to
a) edify the church.
b) express our innermost feelings to God.
c) reveal Christ to the world.

12 Which of these words can also be translated as *worship* in various Scripture passages?
a) Humility
b) Salvation
c) Service
d) Faithfulness

13 Tongues, interpretation, and prophecy are called
a) utterance gifts.
b) miracle gifts.
c) ministry gifts.
d) power gifts.

14 The purpose of the gifts of the Spirit is to glorify Christ and
a) edify the church.
b) meet spiritual needs of unbelievers.
c) develop spiritual leaders in the church.
d) fight against evil.

15 Tongues spoken in public are
a) forbidden by Scripture.
b) the most important spiritual gift.
c) to be followed by an interpretation.
d) sometimes understood by the speaker.

16 The most essential of the power gifts is the gift of
a) healing.
b) faith.
c) prophecy.
d) working of miracles.

17 Another term for *fruit of the Spirit* is
a) Christian character.
b) soul-winning.
c) pastors, teachers, and evangelists.
d) personality traits.

18 Which of these is the best evidence of what I am?
a) Prophesying
b) Possessing the fruit of the Spirit
c) Having the power gifts
d) Christian service

19 The only thing that will be of profit to me when I stand before Christ is
a) my Christian character (love).
b) how many people I have won to Christ.
c) how many years I have served God.
d) my use of spiritual gifts bestowed upon me.

20 Which of these is NOT a reward of fruit-bearing?
a) It is timeless.
b) It brings Christian maturity.
c) It prevents trials in daily life.
d) It brings fullness.

END OF REQUIREMENTS FOR UNIT THREE. Follow the remaining instructions on your answer sheet and return it to your ICI instructor or office in your area. This completes your study of this course. Ask your ICI instructor to recommend another course of study for you.

COUNSELOR, TEACHER, AND GUIDE

ANSWER SHEET FOR UNIT ONE

CS3331

Congratulations on finishing your study of the lessons in Unit One! Please fill in all the blanks below.

Your Name ....

Your ICI Student Number ....

(Leave blank if you do not know what it is.)

Your Mailing Address ....

City .... Province or State ....

Country ....

Age .... Sex .... Occupation ....

Are you married? .... How many members are in your family? ......

How many years have you studied in school? ....

Are you a member of a church? ....

If so, what is the name of the church? ....

What responsibility do you have in your church? ....

....

How are you studying this course: Alone? ....

In a group? ....

What other ICI courses have you studied? ....

....

....

ANSWER SHEET FOR UNIT ONE

Blacken the correct space for each numbered item. For all questions, be sure the number beside the spaces on the answer sheet is the same as the number of the question.

1	A	B	C	D	8	A	B	C	D	15	A	B	C	D
2	A	B	C	D	9	A	B	C	D	16	A	B	C	D
3	A	B	C	D	10	A	B	C	D	17	A	B	C	D
4	A	B	C	D	11	A	B	C	D	18	A	B	C	D
5	A	B	C	D	12	A	B	C	D	19	A	B	C	D
6	A	B	C	D	13	A	B	C	D	20	A	B	C	D
7	A	B	C	D	14	A	B	C	D					

Write below any questions you would like to ask your instructor about the lessons.

....

....

....

Now look over this student report answer sheet to be sure you have completed all the questions. Then return it to your ICI instructor or office in your area. The address should be stamped on the copyright page of your study guide.

For ICI Office Use Only

Date .... **Score** ....

Christian Service Program

COUNSELOR, TEACHER, AND GUIDE

ANSWER SHEET FOR UNIT TWO

CS3331

We hope you have enjoyed your study of the lessons in Unit Two! Please fill in all the blanks below.

Your Name ....

Your ICI Student Number ....

(Leave blank if you do not know what it is.)

Your Mailing Address ....

City .... Province or State ....

Country ....

ANSWER SHEET FOR UNIT TWO

Blacken the correct space for each numbered item. For all questions, be sure the number beside the spaces on the answer sheet is the same as the number of the question.

1	A	B	C	D	8	A	B	C	D	15	A	B	C	D
2	A	B	C	D	9	A	B	C	D	16	A	B	C	D
3	A	B	C	D	10	A	B	C	D	17	A	B	C	D
4	A	B	C	D	11	A	B	C	D	18	A	B	C	D
5	A	B	C	D	12	A	B	C	D	19	A	B	C	D
6	A	B	C	D	13	A	B	C	D	20	A	B	C	D
7	A	B	C	D	14	A	B	C	D					

Write below any questions you would like to ask your instructor about the lessons.

....

....

....

Now look over this student report answer sheet to be sure you have completed all the questions. Then return it to your ICI instructor or office in your area. The address should be stamped on the copyright page of your study guide.

For ICI Office Use Only

Date .... **Score** ....

Christian Service Program

COUNSELOR, TEACHER, AND GUIDE

ANSWER SHEET FOR UNIT THREE

CS3331

We hope you have enjoyed your study of the lessons in Unit Three! Please fill in all the blanks below.

Your Name ....

Your ICI Student Number ....

(Leave blank if you do not know what it is.)

Your Mailing Address ....

City .... Province or State ....

Country ....

REQUEST FOR INFORMATION

The ICI office in your area will be happy to send you information about other ICI courses that are available and their cost. You may use the space below to ask for that information.

....

....

....

ANSWER SHEET FOR UNIT THREE

Blacken the correct space for each numbered item. For all questions, be sure the number beside the spaces on the answer sheet is the same as the number of the question.

1	A	B	C	D	8	A	B	C	D	15	A	B	C	D
2	A	B	C	D	9	A	B	C	D	16	A	B	C	D
3	A	B	C	D	10	A	B	C	D	17	A	B	C	D
4	A	B	C	D	11	A	B	C	D	18	A	B	C	D
5	A	B	C	D	12	A	B	C	D	19	A	B	C	D
6	A	B	C	D	13	A	B	C	D	20	A	B	C	D
7	A	B	C	D	14	A	B	C	D					

Please write below one specific comment about the unit:

....

....

....

CONGRATULATIONS!

You have finished this Christian Service course. We have enjoyed having you as a student and hope you will study more courses with ICI. Return this unit student report answer sheet to your ICI instructor or office in your area. You will then receive your grade on a student score report form along with a certificate or seal for this course in your program of studies.

Please print your name below as you want it on your certificate.

Name ....

For ICI Office Use Only

Date .... **Score** ....